Collected Poems

Collected Poems
1950–1970

Donald Davie

Oxford University Press

New York

1972

First published 1972
by Routledge & Kegan Paul Ltd
Broadway House, 68-74 Carter Lane,
London EC4V 5EL
Printed in Great Britain by
The Camelot Press Ltd, London and Southampton
© Donald Davie 1972

LCN 72-82671

Contents

v

A Winter Talent and Other Poems (1957)

ix

Poems of 1962–3

Los Angeles Poems (1968–9)

Recent Poems

Foreword

It is usual for a writer to say of his first *Collected Poems* that
the book includes 'all those poems that the author wishes to
preserve'. There are two reasons why I do not say this.
In the first place, there are poems published in periodicals
which I have lost sight of, and so they have not been looked
at as candidates for inclusion. And in the second place,
more crucially, I have not wanted to fudge the record by
wisdom after the event. Accordingly, I have reprinted every
poem that has appeared in my previous collections, except
in the rather special cases of my adaptations of Mickiewicz
and my translations from Pasternak; and have amplified
the record by reprinting from periodicals and miscellanies
certain poems which I liked and could put my hands on.
This does not mean that I am complacently happy about
every poem I have committed to print between hard covers,
but simply that I believe I ought to stand on my record,
such as it is. For the same reason I've taken pains to present
the poems to the reader in the chronological order they
were composed in, so far as I can be sure of that;
the chronological order is reliable, if not month by month,
at least year by year.

As a record of twenty years of published writing, the
collection (I hope) reveals a development from first to last
which is more than a sterile alternation or an eclectic snatching
and grabbing, more too than nervous response to the winds of
fashion. I'll be particularly glad if some of my English
readers in particular discern a movement from first to last
which in some way parallels a development over the same
period which they can discern in themselves. But this sounds as
if I were writing only for my contemporaries, and I hope
that isn't so.

Some of the poems, especially the earlier ones, are a great
deal more obscure than I meant them to be; and in those
cases I've apologetically, if lamely, tried to clarify matters in
some brief notes.

Acknowledgments

The author and publishers wish to thank the following for kind permission to reproduce the works cited, or extracts from them:

London Magazine Editions for *Six Epistles to Eva Hesse*

The Manchester University Press for 'March', 'Fairy Story', 'The Miracle' and 'Magdalene' from *The Poems of Doctor Zhivago*

The Marvell Press for *The Forests of Lithuania* and *A Sequence for Francis Parkman*

Poetry for 'On Not Deserving', 'Autumn Imagined', 'Hot Hands', 'Where Depths are Surfaces' and 'Vying'

The Wesleyan University Press for *New and Selected Poems* and *Events and Wisdoms*

Homage to William Cowper

Mrs Throckmorton's bull-finch sang a song.
(Domesticate that comfortable bird!)
But still the deer has wandered from the herd,
The bard was not articulate for long.

A pasticheur of late-Augustan styles,
I too have sung the sofa and the hare,
Made nightmare ride upon a private air
And hearths, extinguished, send a chill for miles.

This costive plan, this dense upholstery,
These mice and kittens, this constrictive rhyme,
These small Infernos of another time –
What's all this modish Hecuba to me?

Most poets let the morbid fancy roam.
The squalid rat broke through the finch's fence,
Which was a cage, and still was no defence:
For Horror starts, like Charity, at home.

At Knaresborough

'Broad acres, sir.' You hear them in my talk.
As tell-tale as a pigment in the skin,
Vowels as broad as all the plain of York
Proclaim me of this country and your kin.

And, gratified to have your guess endorsed,
You warm to me. I thaw, and am approved.
But, to be frank, the sentiment is forced,
When I pretend, for your sake, to be moved.

To feel so little, when his sympathies
Would be so much engaged (he would have said),
Surprised the poet too. But there it is,
The heart is not to be solicited.

I

Believe me, sir, I only ply my trade,
Which is to know when I am played upon.
You might have moved, you never shall persuade.
You grow too warm. I must be moving on.

The Bride of Reason

Pragmatical old Capulet, the head,
So long has ruled, or seemed to rule, the heart,
That Juliet muse, to County Paris wed,
Lets his good sense determine all her art.

Charmed with his manners towards alternatives,
The unacceptable Romeos she has kissed,
The heart with this judicious husband lives,
And, wed to Reason, seems a moralist.

Some who have loved the lady are dismayed;
Some who have loved her first love, Romeo,
Think that impulsive gallant is betrayed,
Now Juliet's voice is so demure and low.

Only her father thinks the wench is sly,
And sees in her docility her treason;
She loves the truth he thought she must deny,
Her lyric to the music of his reason.

Brides of Reason (1955)

Among Artisans' Houses

High above Plymouth, not so high
But that the roof-tops seem to sweat
In the damp sea-mist, the damp sea-sky
Lowers on terraced houses, set
Like citadels, so blank and high;
Clothes-lines run to a handy cleat,
And plots are furiously neat.

There are not many notice this
Resourcefulness of citizens,
And few esteem it. But it is
An outcome of the civil sense,
Its small and mean utilities;
A civilization, in its way,
Its rudiments or its decay.

And if civility is gone,
As we assume it is, the moulds
Of commonwealth all broken down,
Then how explain that this still holds,
The strong though cramped and cramping tone
Of mutual respect, that cries
Out of these small civilities?

It could occur, perhaps, only here,
On these hills over Plymouth Sound,
Where continuity is clear
From Drake to now, where life is bound
Still, though obscurely, to the gear
Traditionally maritime,
And sanctioned by the use of time.

There is no moral to the scene,
Curious relic from the past.
What has and not what might have been
It serves to show now. And at last,
Shortly, nothing will be seen
By which historians may fix
The moral shape of politics.

Three Moral Discoveries

I

Oh I can praise a cloistered virtue, such
As knows it cannot fear itself too much;
That though innate corruption breaks the laws,
Woman, for instance, is the efficient cause.
The genuine prayer, when all is said and done,
Is 'Lead us not into temptation'.

II

As Will and I went down the hill
Who should we meet, dressed up to kill,
  But a sexual misdemeanour.

When Will and I got into the train,
There was the loose-limbed wench again,
  An inconsiderate action.

As I left the station, I missed my pipe,
And I turned on Will. He began to weep.

It wasn't until I was nearly thirty,
I noticed the will resents being dirty.

III

I dared occasion, and came off intact,
Unharmed, not therefore unashamed. The act
Is unimportant; and the times I fell
In fact, in thought, in wish, in all but will,
Reflect how little credit falls to me,
At fault just there, in will's obduracy.

Twilight on the Waste Lands

Some quickly-weathering rock, perhaps,
Eroded by a sandy wind,
Conceals a carving, in the lapse
Of centuries so often skinned
That more than patinas escape,

And from the crag the chiselled shape
Disperses on the desert wind.

The traveller, at dusk or dawn,
Adverted by a trick of light,
Starts at a meaning, hints a form
So fugitive, the doubtful sight
Suspects no hand of man at all,
An artefact so natural
It seems the work of air and light.

Conceive of such a poem, planned
With such a nicety of touch
It quite conceals the maker's hand
And seems a votive fragment, such
As patient scholars make unclear
And, hazarding their guesses, fear
They have read into it too much.

Strung to the dominant, the voice
Guys all the intervals of speech.
Time-honoured forms present a choice
Of parody or else pastiche.
In all but what seems inchoate
We quiz the past. To see it straight
Requires a form just out of reach:

Such form as, see, the setting sun
Behind the shoulder of the bluff
Brings out there! But the beam is gone;
Old Rocky-face there in the rough,
Asleep again, has wiped the slate,
A God, a shape, that must await
A light that's sensitive enough.

Sand-blast the friable. Concede
Skin after skin, but frayed, not flayed,
Not chipped to chastened bone, but freed
From every play but light and shade,
Invertebrate. The marble chills;
Be no more shapely than the hills.
See, there again, the sense betrayed!

Demi-Exile. Howth

Daisy and dandelion, speedwell, daffodil,
Lean from the parks on this sea-ward hill,
In Queen Victoria's Anglo-Ireland,
Lean from the lawns to my English hand
In Anglo-India, Anglo-Ireland,
Cities drowning in drifted sand.

Division of loyalties, dolour of exile,
Do you command a quizzical smile
Here, at the roof that once defended
Jonathan Swift's demented head?
Here, in the suburb that Hopkins visited,
Strangled in sand of its famous dead?

Flowers of England, flowers of Ireland,
Lean from earth to my empty hand.
Hands acknowledging no allegiance,
Gloved for good against brutal chance,
Pluck the shadow and not the substance,
Grasp no nettle of circumstance.

Hypochondriac Logic

Appendicitis is his worst
Obsession, mordant from the first
And unannounced. For who but he,
By curious failing schooled to see
The tiniest pain, can hope to be
Fore-warned of appendectomy?
So thinking, he thinks pain to be
More real as more illusory.

So argue all men who have thought
A truth more true as more remote,
Or in poetic worlds confide
The more their air is rarefied.

This the Shelleyan failing is,
Who feared elephantiasis,
Whose poems infect his readers too,
Who, since they're vague, suppose them true.

But lagging down a crippled street
Like fugitives from their own feet,
Some who are whole can yet observe
Disease is what we all deserve,
Or else disdain a painless life
While any squeal beneath the knife.
So, if you trace the impulse back,
The best are hypochondriac.

So poets may astonish you
With what is not, but should be, true,
And shackle on a moral shape
You only thought you could escape;
And if their scenery is queer,
Its prototype may not be here,
Unless inside a frightened mind,
Which may be dazzled, but not blind.

Creon's Mouse

Creon, I think, could never kill a mouse
When once that dangerous girl was put away,
Shut up unbridled in her rocky house,
Colossal nerve denied the light of day.

Now Europe's hero, the humaner King
Who hates himself, is humanized by shame,
Is he a curbed or a corroded spring?
A will that's bent, or buckled? Tense, or tame?

If too much daring brought (he thought) the war,
When that was over nothing else would serve
But no one must be daring any more,
A self-induced and stubborn loss of nerve.

In itching wainscot having met his match,
He waits unnerved, and hears his caverned doom,
The nausea that struggles to dispatch
Pink-handed horror in a craggy room.

The absolute endeavour was the catch;
To clean the means and never mind the end
Meant he had not to chasten but to scotch
The will he might have managed to amend.

You that may think yourselves not proud at all,
Learn this at least from humble Creon's fall:
The will that is subjèct, not overthrown,
Is humbled by some power not its own.

Poem as Abstract

'To write about a tree . . . you must first *be* a tree.' (W. R. Rodgers)

I

A poem is less an orange than a grid;
It hoists a charge; it does not ooze a juice.
It has no rind, being entirely hard.

All drumming yards and open, it asserts
That clouds have way upon them, and that hills
Breast into time behind a singing strut.

A sheer abstraction, apt upon the grass
Of London parks, has emulated oak
And aped the ramage that it could surpass.

That construct, ribbed with wire across a quern,
Is caging such serenity of stress
As boughs, or fruit that breaks them, cannot learn.

For gods are gathered from the styles they wear,
And do they curl, a fœtus in a fruit,
Or, like Orion, pinned upon the air?

10

No trowelled matron but a rigger's mate,
The pile-high poet has no time to brood.
He steps the mast; it does not germinate.

Not for ingestion but to frame the air
He flies the spar that even winter's tree
In green ambition cannot grow so spare.

The orange dangles, drops, and comes again.
To make a fruit he has to be a fruit,
A globe of pulp about a pip of pain.

But tip-toe cages lofted in a day
(To make a grid he has to *make* a grid)
Have come unprecedented, and to stay.

If poems make a style, a way of walking
With enterprise, should not a poet's gait
Be counties-wide, this stride, the pylons stalking?

Mamertinus on Rhetoric, A.D. 291

Personae seek provisional assent.
Perversities of unforeseen address
Obliquely murmur, and a sentiment
Finds not expression but expressiveness.

This is the entry of the chamberlains
To Dioclesian and his fictive son.
They speak through masks. The double image feigns
To share the dye too dangerous for one.

Urbanities of Danube and Milan
(Himself at Nicomedia, at York
Constantius Chlorus) baffle, if they can,
And drown the edict in a buzz of talk.

But virtue has to rule the world alone
And scorns assistance from a trick of light,
Her ceremonies rectitude, her tone
Not florid nor austere, but coming right.

A poor decorum? So it seems, my lord,
There in your palace planted like a camp.
The Roman style, however, can afford
To think seven hills an all-sufficient ramp.

Evening on the Boyne

The Boyne at Navan swam in light,
Where children headlong through the trees
Plunged down the sward, and nicked the bright
Precarious evening with unease.

Swans at the bottom of a vale,
Sailing rapidly from sight,
Made the sweet arrangements fail
And emptied all the precious light.

A moment later all was well,
The light was full, the ranks were closed;
The fields of flags, the wading mill
Withdrew again, once more composed.

But what happened? Who had made
This mirror tremble and subside?
The evening by what eye betrayed
Winced, like a curtain drawn aside?

The shutter of some active mind,
Panicked by a glide of swans,
Closing, made all nature blind,
Then photographed itself at once.

O bleak and lunar emptiness,
How many eyes were then belied?
A god's, a man's, a swan's, and – yes,
The very flags were iris-eyed!

Thyestes

Brush of a raven's, not an eagle's wing!
No wonder older classicists could wish
For something more cathartic than this King
Who spooned his baked-meat children from a dish.

With Jung and Frazer, Tylor, Graves and Lang,
The scholiast can wash the blood away.
But what's the use? The savage poets sang
Enormities that happen every day.

No talons raven in a titan's gut
When dreadful fathers of a fortnight's date
Are drowning kittens in a water-butt.
But see, a baby's finger in the plate!

Belfast on a Sunday Afternoon

Visiting Belfast at the end of June,
We found the Orange Lodge behind a band:
Sashes and bearskins in the afternoon,
White cotton gloves upon a crippled hand.

Pastmasters pale, elaborately grim,
Marched each alone, beneath a bowler hat:
And, catapulted on a crumpled limb,
A lame man leapt the tram-lines like a bat.

And first of all we tried to laugh it off,
Acting bemusement in the grimy sun;
But stayed to worry where we came to scoff,
As loud contingents followed, one by one.

Pipe bands, flute bands, brass bands and silver bands,
Presbyter's pibroch and the deacon's serge,
Came stamping where the iron Mænad stands,
Victoria, glum upon a grassy verge.

Some brawny striplings sprawled upon the lawn;
No man is really crippled by his hates.
Yet I remembered with a sudden scorn
Those 'passionate intensities' of Yeats.

Zip!

I'd have the silence like a heavy chock
That's kicked away as you begin to read;
And sense, responding to the tiny shock,
Roll forward, fire, and smoothly gather speed.

Lines should be hoops that, vibrantly at rest,
Devolve like cables as the switches trip,
Each syllable entailing all the rest,
And rhymes that strike, exploding like a whip.

I'd have the spark that leaps upon the gun
By one short fuse, electrically clear;
And all be done before you've well begun.
(It is reverberations that you hear.)

On Bertrand Russell's 'Portraits from Memory'

Those Cambridge generations, Russell's, Keynes' . . .
And mine? Oh mine was Wittgenstein's, no doubt:
Sweet pastoral, too, when some-one else explains,
Although my memories leave the eclogues out.

The clod's not bowed by sedentary years,
Yet, set by Thyrsis, he's a crippled man:
How singularly naked each appears,
Beside the other on this bosky plan.

Arrangements of the copse and cloister seem,
Although effective, still Utopian,
For groves find room, behind a leafy screen,
For sage and harvester, but not for man.

I wonder still which of the hemispheres
Infects the other, in this grassy globe;
The chumbling moth of Madingley, that blears
The labourer's lamp, destroys the scarlet robe.

It was the Muse that could not make her home
In that too thin and yet too sluggish air,
Too volatile to live among the loam,
Her sheaves too heavy for the talkers there.

The Garden Party

Above a stretch of still unravaged weald
In our Black Country, in a cedar-shade,
I found, shared out in tennis courts, a field
Where children of the local magnates played.

And I grew envious of their moneyed ease
In Scott Fitzgerald's unembarrassed vein.
Let prigs, I thought, fool others as they please,
I only wish I had my time again.

To crown a situation as contrived
As any in 'The Beautiful and Damned',
The phantom of my earliest love arrived;
I shook absurdly as I shook her hand.

As dusk drew in on cultivated cries,
Faces hung pearls upon a cedar-bough;
And gin could blur the glitter of her eyes,
But it's too late to learn to tango now.

My father, of a more submissive school,
Remarks the rich themselves are always sad.
There is that sort of equalizing rule;
But theirs is all the youth we might have had.

The Owl Minerva

The muse that makes pretensions to discourse,
Not sage nor sybil but a piece of both,
Astute in form, oracular in force,
Can make a proposition sound an oath.

Rapid, abrupt and violent like a blow,
An exclamation or ecstatic howl,
Still it asserts, and shows it is not so,
Articulates the hooting of an owl.

Can spells or riddles be articulate?
We take our stand, to make the music heard,
And only speech aspires to music's state.
The Owl Minerva was no singing bird.

Heart Beats

If music be the muses' paragon,
Where mostly pure relation is expressed,
The poet looks accusingly upon
This cramped performer drumming in his breast.

'Why brag,' he cries, 'of buffetings survived
To make the high-pitched harmonies of strain?
You suffered, but some colder thing contrived,
Articulated, and endorsed the pain.'

As from a cellar, unrepentant comes
The virtuoso's lunatic tattoo,
Beating to parley in a school of drums:
'I plot the passions, and endure them too.'

Machineries of Shame

Decaying teeth, before they start to ache,
Start up obscure machineries of shame,
As if the mind were fool enough to take
This, and the soul's corruption, for the same.

This is to make debility a crime;
So, too, a mere discomfiture can start
A blush as hot as, at another time,
A black place in the mouth or in the heart, –

And justly, too. Guilt, sleeping in the cell,
Sparks out upon the throwing of a switch.
If sins can do it, blunders serve as well,
And jumping nerves can make a conscience twitch.

Pushkin. A Didactic Poem

'he did not yet know well those hidden mechanisms of the
person by which it achieves its isolation from others and
withdraws into itself; he was entirely surrendered to his genius,
disarmed by his own power; and if his pride led him to
challenge God, he cancelled by that very act his own right to
deny Him.' (WLADIMIR WEIDLÉ)

What with hounds and friends and, in the winter,
Skating, he was seldom bored.
He had learned to be wary, was at pains, I think,
To remain amused?

In the matter of Pushkin, Emily Brontë
Is the best analogy in some ways
Among our poets. As in her verse,
In Pushkin's we assume the truth
That for life to be tolerable, man must
Be wary, ingenious, quick to change
Among diversions, grave or frivolous,
To keep off spleen; although for her,
As she was a woman, a narrower range
Presented itself, and so she is less
Various, flexible, fiery, though as noble
As Pushkin was, more stoical.

Pushkin's draughts-playing and his drinking,
His friends, his travelling, even some
Of his mistresses, he considered as
So many improvisations against
Boredom. But the boredom was
No vacancy nor want of occupation
Nor lack of resources. It was the spleen,

And Pushkin certainly fled before it
Or circumvented it. His poems
Record the circumventions as
Hours when the mind, turned outwards, knew
Friendships or the approach of death
As gifts. The poet exhibits here
How to be conscious in every direction
But that of the self, where deception starts.
This is nobility; not lost
Wholly perhaps, if lost to art.

Grateful tears, delicious sorrow,
Said the Russian gentleman,
Mozart will be dead tomorrow
Of this confusion.

As Byron said of Keats, 'I don't
mean he is indecent, but
viciously soliciting
his own ideas.'

(Schiller and Dostoievsky, oysters
Pearling their own disease, the saints
Full of self-help)

Long before Shakespeare wrote, or Donne,
In the modern manner, there were minds
Aware of themselves, and figuring this
In psychomachia. But the Greeks
Knew states of innocence, the will
Turned always outwards, courage the gift
Counting for virtue, and control,
As of the craven self, a notion
Lost in the social usage. Thus

Self-consciousness is not at fault
In itself. It can be kept
Other than morbid, under laws
Of disciplined sensibility, such
As the seventeenth-century Wit.
But all such disciplines depend
On disciplines of social use,
Now widely lost. Yet there are those
Few men remaining, gifted, or
Especially heroic, or,
Like Pushkin, brilliantly both.
Ask when we are diseased, and these
Will answer: When the moral will
Intervenes to sap the heart,
When the difficult feelings are
Titillated and confused
For novel combinations, or
Ransacked for virtue.

Remains the voice that moves on silence
In moral commonplace, where yet
Some thwart and stern communal sense
Whispers, before we all forget.

What need dissection of the thrust
Which motivates the skating feet,
When that can always be deduced
From the figure of eight?

What need dissection of the thrust
Which motivates the skating feet?
Skating with friends in the winter,
He foretold our defeat.

At the Synod in St Patrick's

This head meant to be massive and therefore,
Being a woman's, less than beautiful,
Is, being young and animated, more
Engaging than a less emphatic skull.

Late flowering, like a cleft-encompassed bush,
To this tradition time has left behind,
Can it be long before her fibres push
At barren rock, the backward-looking mind?

Yet, mollified not merely by their youth,
The jowl too full, the brows like heavy eaves
Bespeak, within, the climate of the truth,
Like Eden's crags with honey in their caves.

The bland and sparkling weather of the good
Extends its dry elation, and disarms
Across two pews my Lucifer that would
Learn why such light should sadden as it charms.

Remembering the 'Thirties

I

Hearing one saga, we enact the next.
We please our elders when we sit enthralled;
But then they're puzzled; and at last they're vexed
To have their youth so avidly recalled.

It dawns upon the veterans after all
That what for them were agonies, for us
Are high-brow thrillers, though historical;
And all their feats quite strictly fabulous.

This novel written fifteen years ago,
Set in my boyhood and my boyhood home,
These poems about 'abandoned workings', show
Worlds more remote than Ithaca or Rome.

The Anschluss, Guernica – all the names
At which those poets thrilled or were afraid
For me mean schools and schoolmasters and games;
And in the process some-one is betrayed.

Ourselves perhaps. The Devil for a joke
Might carve his own initials on our desk,
And yet we'd miss the point because he spoke
An idiom too dated, Audenesque.

Ralegh's Guiana also killed his son.
A pretty pickle if we came to see
The tallest story really packed a gun,
The Telemachiad an Odyssey.

II

Even to them the tales were not so true
As not to be ridiculous as well;
The ironmaster met his Waterloo,
But Rider Haggard rode along the fell.

'Leave for Cape Wrath tonight!' They lounged away
On Fleming's trek or Isherwood's ascent.
England expected every man that day
To show his motives were ambivalent.

They played the fool, not to appear as fools
In time's long glass. A deprecating air
Disarmed, they thought, the jeers of later schools;
Yet irony itself is doctrinaire,

And curiously, nothing now betrays
Their type to time's derision like this coy
Insistence on the quizzical, their craze
For showing Hector was a mother's boy.

A neutral tone is nowadays preferred.
And yet it may be better, if we must,
To praise a stance impressive and absurd
Than not to see the hero for the dust.

For courage is the vegetable king,
The sprig of all ontologies, the weed
That beards the slag-heap with his hectoring,
Whose green adventure is to run to seed.

The Evangelist

'My brethren . . .' And a bland, elastic smile
Basks on the mobile features of Dissent.
No hypocrite, you understand. The style
Befits a church that's based on sentiment.

Solicitations of a swirling gown,
The sudden vox humana, and the pause,
The expert orchestration of a frown
Deserve, no doubt, a murmur of applause.

The tides of feeling round me rise and sink;
Bunyan, however, found a place for wit.
Yes, I am more persuaded than I think;
Which is, perhaps, why I disparage it.

You round upon me, generously keen:
The man, you say, is patently sincere.
Because he is so eloquent, you mean?
That test was never patented, my dear.

If, when he plays upon our sympathies,
I'm pleased to be fastidious, and you
To be inspired, the vice in it is this:
Each does us credit, and we know it too.

An English Revenant

I

From easterly crepuscular arrivals
Come with me by the self-consuming north
(The North is spirit), to the loam-foot west
And opulent departures of the south.

You that went north for geysers or for grouse,
While Pullman sleepers lulled your sleeping head,
You never saw my mutilated house
Flame in the north by Sheffield as you fled.

You that went west, young man, behind the range
('Westward the course of Empire takes its way')
You never knew my west that cannot change
Its stolid dream and violent feet of clay.

And what became of Waring in the east?
He learnt what traitors generous feelings are,
And lost his nerve, and knew no Samarcand,
In Vishnu-land no hopeful Avatar.

But in the nub of war, a sullen soldier,
He saw the south, its orchards and its wine;
A rich wrap slipping from a Mayfair shoulder,
Successful chromium on his future shine.

In passing, be it understood
Most revenants are flesh and blood.

II

My home is in the west,
But not in the far west;
And though I was born in the north,
It was not in the far north;
I am lately returned from the east,
But from the middle east;
My songs aspire to the south,
But not to the deep south.

I have cured my breast
Of its need for action;
I have taught it to rest
This side of the Western passes;
Its deeds are commendable,
Not noble.

I have laughed my mind
Out of its need for abstraction;
I have taught it not to find
Shrines in the Orient;
Its thoughts are in tune with the time;
They are not exalted.

I have cheated my will
Out of its need for command;
I have taught it not to kill
Free water into ice;
Its ways are adaptable,
Not unswerving.

Now only my singing mouth
Thirsts for the springs of the south.

III

A craning lamb that craves an empty dug;
A murdered trunk still twitching on the ground;
A water-wheel inertly turning round
Beneath a stream that would not fill a jug.

Such mere momentum moves me still to you,
Supposed a court, a region of reward;
Cannot this wreck of compasses afford
Some south at last, deserved, and coming true?

'My country 'tis of thee . . .' What can I say?
'Gone in the teeth,' sang Owen and Sassoon,
Or Ezra Pound who parodied their tune.
'London, Thou art of townes A per se.'

It is, my dear, an intimate inquires
(Indigenous, with hard provincial mouth),
What news of all the olives of the south,
Since Owen's bugles blew from saddened shires?

England, we wheel and fly about you still,
The dead of that and of another war.
It is a laurel we are looking for,
Or bounty of the horn we thought to fill.

Hawkshead and Dachau in a Christmas Glass

At home with my infirmities I fare
Forth to the nightfall on bald avenues,
Whose charities I shall no more refuse,
However cheaply on the blue-black air
Proffered from lighted windows, such as once,
Though more sporadic, from the mountain-road
      Welcomed, where Hawkshead glowed.
    Panels of domestic light!
    Like labels pasted on the night,
    (Pasted, opaque, rectangular,
Cut out of paper like a tinsel star –)
I see the sleigh that rocks, the bells that chime
Upon the plate-glass of suburban groceries,
Flatly announcing coming Christmas-time,
The holy time honoured in parodies.

II

When Hawkshead's poet chose to be humane
And praise the homestead beaming from afar
His Michael's cottage was 'The Evening Star',
      An elevated strain –
Oh Wordsworth! when we walked the mountain-road
So long ago, in quite another mood
    We crested every contour of the fell,
Dark-blue and frost-white on the darker blue,
Our spirits swelling with the upland swell
To bulky heights and knolls we never knew.
Now these lean trees, over the parkland wall,
    Delicate brush-work on a darkling ground;
That deep blue ground that, feathered by the tall
And springing brushes, seems a felted pall;
Its matt and nap as dense as if it lay
A shielding wing over the sharpest day;
    I see the aspirations they invite,
    I lean towards, but dare not launch in flight.

III

As I shall not aspire
To wear the coat of fire
Which (we have proved) incinerates the heart;
Because the human mind
Cannot be far refined,
But must admit its grossness from the start;
I hope for no dark elbow-room, to win
Accommodation with the night within.

IV

Making these faces in a Christmas glass
May terrify some others as they pass;
For window-gazers, when a God is dead,
Abide no dreamed-up artefact of mind,
But by reflection from a human head
When most it lacks divinity, they find,
That is, invent, perfection in its stead.
For not by what we want is God defined,
Only by what we lack;
By what is wanting to us; what we need,
Not what we know we need. And at our back
His eye augments our window-shopping greed.

V

Insatiable proud buyers who could rest
With nothing but the best,
Who pressed through to the other side
Of every flaring window, and defied
Tragedy even to reflect them right,
Still asked too little, and at best supplied
Only their aspirations. Far too bright
A light shone through the glass; their dazzled sight
Losing the lens, they put us in a fright,
Claiming it was God's face they brought to light.
Outside the bleakest pane,
Bulging like water in a rippled glass,
My face makes such pretensions as surpass
Insane self-deified
Projectors of a private pantheon,

Purveyors' voices from the other side
Of window-panes that heaven was pasted on.

VI

There was a time I would have scorned to think
My self-aversions so entirely eased
By neighbour windows. Such a night of ink
Required, I thought, supernal light at least.
To be believers, let us not forget
How cheaply all our petty needs are met,
All that we know of. If we blow them up
And push away the off-hand proffered cup,
   Each time we raise our price
Some unimagined need is given up,
And we are gulled, intending to be nice.
In such a time, antediluvian,
We came to Hawkshead. It was long ago,
In our own youth and in the youth of Man,
Not long ago in years, but since we know
At Dachau Man's maturity began
And that was earlier, it was long ago,
A time we could not easily outgrow.
At Dachau Yeats and Rilke died. We found,
   In those who lived before,
Our growing pains. A groaning, cracking sound,
Exploding now through each exclusive store,
Starred what we thought light of uncommon day
And damned it glass. Yet some endured the ray,
Wordsworth for one, who may have hoped for light
That never was on sea or land, but knew
The brittle thing that he was looking through,
A waving pane projected on the night.

VII

No wind, please God, will rise tonight. The trees
Still sprig the velvet on the pelt of night.
Still, stuck about the raw estate, one sees
The coloured labels of a Christmas light.
Still, in the stillness, only smoke aspires.
(The movement in the stillness is not ours.)

We shut up shop, and there's
No glimmer now by which to see the wares
Banked behind glass; but in the early hours
Some mooning hobo, by inhuman fires
Of stars or moon, may, glancing in the glass,
Observe his insufficiencies, and find
A supplement there hinted, to surpass
The dearest purchase that he had in mind.

      Natural pieties,
      Unthought-of charities
Grow up about the newest housing-scheme;
      Curtained or not, the light
      Is tempered to our sight,
And poorest taste can dress the dearest theme,
Where cotton-wool can simulate the snow
And coloured bulbs make Bethlehem a show.

Eight Years After

If distance lends enchantment to the view,
Enormities should not be scrutinized.
What's true of white, holds of black magic too;
And, indistinct, evil is emphasized.

Gilfillan, telling how the poet Churchill
'Indulged in nameless orgies', makes us smile;
We think such large unutterables fill
Vapid lacunæ in a frowzy style.

A case however can be made for this:
The queasy Levite need not be ashamed
To have no stomach for atrocities.
We brook them better, once they have been named.

For fearsome issues, being squarely faced,
Grow fearsomely familiar. To name
Is to acknowledge. To acquire the taste
Comes on the heels of honouring the claim.

'Let nothing human be outside my range.'
Yet horrors named make exorcisms fail:
A thought once entertained is never strange,
But who forgets the face 'beyond the pale'?

Selina, Countess of Huntingdon

Your special witness, as I recollect,
Was, in your fervour, elegance; you yearned
For Grace, but only gracefully, and earned,
By sheer good taste, the title of 'elect'.

So perfectly well-bred that in your hands
All pieties were lavender, that scent
Lingered about your college, where you spent
Your fragrance on the burly ordinands.

In your communion, virtue was uncouth;
But now that rigour lost its cutting edge,
As charm in you drove its schismatic wedge
Between your church's beauty and its truth.

Method. For Ronald Gaskell

For such a theme (atrocities) you find
My style, you say, too neat and self-possessed.
I ought to show a more disordered mind.

But Wesley's sermons could be methodized
According to a Ramist paradigm;
Enthusiasts can never be surprised.

The method in the madness of their zeal
Discounts their laceration of the wounds
That, though so bloodied, have had time to heal.

Cassandra plays her frenzied part too well
To be convincing in hysteria.
Has discourse still its several heads, in Hell?

It has, of course; and why conceal the fact?
An even tenor's sensitive to shock,
And stains spread furthest where the floor's not cracked.

Woodpigeons at Raheny

One simple and effective rhyme
Over and over in the April light;
    And a touch of the old time
In the serving-man, stooping, aproned tight,
At the end of the dappled avenue
To the easy phrase, 'tereu-tereu',
Mulled over by the sleepy dove –
This was the poem I had to write.

White wall where the creepers climb
Year after year on the sunny side;
    And a touch of the old time
In the sandalled Capuchin's silent stride
Over the shadows and through the clear
Cushion-soft wooing of the ear
From two meadows away, by the dove –
This was the poem that was denied.

For whether it was the friar's crime,
His lean-ness suddenly out of tune;
    Or a touch of the old time
In the given phrase, with its unsought boon
Of a lax autumnal atmosphere,
Seemed quaint and out of keeping here,
I do not know. I know the dove
Outsang me down the afternoon.

Love-Poems: for Mairi MacInnes

from *Poets of the 1950s* (1955)

All these love-poems . . .!
Love in its place
Is simple, therefore interesting;
Inscrutable face,
Looming through leaves or water,
Unlooked-for aisle or island.

It is not the whole story,
Nor can stand for such
As 'human relations' in little;
It is not so much
A paradigm as an interruption,
Not to be looked for in a day's travel.

And all these . . .!
Some 'civilized,'
Some frenzied, some 'gravely moving,'
But yours surprised,
Still dazzled in the roasted glade,
Astounded after long days in the forest.

Jacob's Ladder

(*Unpublished*)
It was agreed we would not mount by those
Platonic ladders planted on the heart,
Minds that abide the body and its throes,
Reluctantly, and only for a start.
But Jacob's is a ladder we ascend
Without our knowing any sense of strain,
To upland air that we need not expend
One gulp of carnal breathing to attain.
So here we are upon the heights, my love,
Although in habit's level pastures still.

31

We want, and yet we do not want, the skill
To scale the peaks that others tell us of,
Where breathing gets so difficult, and the will
Kicks back the ground it tries to rise above.

(1955)

A Winter Talent and Other Poems (1957)

Time Passing, Beloved

Time passing, and the memories of love
Coming back to me, carissima, no more mockingly
Than ever before; time passing, unslackening,
Unhastening, steadily; and no more
Bitterly, beloved, the memories of love
Coming into the shore.

How will it end? Time passing and our passages of love
As ever, beloved, blind
As ever before; time binding, unbinding
About us; and yet to remember
Never less chastening, nor the flame of love
Less like an ember.

What will become of us? Time
Passing, beloved, and we in a sealed
Assurance unassailed
By memory. How can it end,
This siege of a shore that no misgivings have steeled,
No doubts defend?

Dream Forest

These have I set up,
Types of ideal virtue,
To be authenticated
By no one's Life and Times,
But by a sculptor's logic

Of whom I have commanded,
To dignify my groves,
Busts in the antique manner,
Each in the space mown down
Under its own sway:

First, or to break the circle,
Brutus, imperious, curbed
Not much by the general will,
But by a will to be curbed,
A preference for limits;

Pushkin next, protean
Who recognised no checks
Yet brooked them all – a mind
Molten and thereby fluent,
Unforced, easily strict;

The next, less fortunate,
Went honourably mad,
The angry annalist
Of hearth and marriage bed,
Strindberg – a staring head.

Classic, romantic, realist,
These have I set up.
These have I set, and a few trees.
When will a grove grow over
This mile upon mile of moor?

Obiter Dicta

Trying to understand myself, I fetch
    My father's image to me. There he is, augmenting
    The treasury of his prudence with a clutch
Of those cold eggs, Great Truths – his scrivener's hand
    Confiding apothegms to his pocket book.
    Does mine do more than snap the elastic band
Of rhyme about them? In an age that teaches
    How pearls of wisdom only look like eggs,
    The tide, afflatus, still piles up on the beaches
Pearls that he prizes, stones that he retrieves
    Misguidedly from poetry's undertow,
    Deaf to the harsh retraction that achieves
Its scuttering backwash, ironies. And yet,
    Recalling his garrulity, I see
    There's method in it. Seeming to forget

The point at issue, the palmer tells his beads,
    Strung by connections nonchalantly weak
    Upon the thread of argument he needs
To bring them through his fingers, round and round,
    Tasting of gristle, savoury; and he hears,
    Like rubbing stones, their dry conclusive sound.

Himself an actor (He can play the clown),
    He knows the poet's a man of parts; the sage
Is one of them, buffoonery like his own,
    Means to an end. So, if he loves the page
That grows sententious with a terse distinction,
    Yet lapidary moralists are dumb
About the precepts that he acts upon,
    Brown with tobacco from his rule of thumb.

'Not bread but a stone!' – the deep-sea fishermen
    Denounce our findings, father. Pebbles, beads,
    Perspicuous dicta, gems from Emerson,
Whatever stands when all about it slides,
    Whatever in the oceanic welter
    Puts period to unpunctuated tides,
These, that we like, they hate. And after all, for you,
    To take but with a pinch of salt to take
    The maxims of the sages is the true
Great Truth of all. To keep, as you would say,
    A sense of proportion, I should portion out
    The archipelago across the bay,
One island to so much sea. Assorted
    Poetic pleasures come in bundles then,
    Strapped up by rhyme, not otherwise supported?

Turning about his various gems to take
    Each other's lustre by a temperate rule,
He walks the graveyard where I have to make
    Not centos but inscriptions, and a whole
That's moved from inward, dancing. Yet I trace
    Among his shored-up epitaphs my own:
Art, as he hints, turns on a commonplace,
    And Death is a tune to dance to, cut in stone.

Mens Sana in Corpore Sano

Certainly, Lean-shanks, you have forced the pace –
In the bath your body shows it; and you have
The right, considering your shrunken hams,
To rock on that notorious see-saw, mind
And body. But you have forced the pace,
Not forced (take heart) that alternating tempo
To an inhuman standstill – forced the flesh
To some four-minute mile, or forced the mind
To play the ruffian pandar to the blood.

Time's gradual and lenient castration
Unfilms the eye and stills the straying hand,
Unstops ear and nostril; and the tongue
Wags to expansive music, that could risk
(So loose it was till lately) only terse
And summary formulations. As for youth,
See where it throngs these garnished avenues
To deck a house under whose ageing beams
The blithe young tenant comes of age tomorrow.

You know the Stoic's one indulgence now,
The wrist that, opened, bleeds into the bath
Crimsoning Time's still water – yet with blood
(The Epicurean's boast) no violence
Has loosed upon yourself, beyond
That something less than suicidal forcing,
The acceleration of the chemistries
Of undeflected change. Prepare to open
All of the body's avenues but its veins.

At the Cradle of Genius

'Not the least enviable of your many gifts,
Being indeed (what seems unfair) implied
In that first bargain, genius, are two
Appurtenances or corollaries:
One which we hope you do not recognize
Or else it halves its value, one we hope you do
By the same token; and we mean

Charm in the first place, in the second
A narrowing of the choice of destinies.

For character may be fate, and yet vocation
(Differing from the casual gift, a flair)
Can so subsume the variants under types
That, all the issues coming clear,
The gift becomes of nothing else but freedom,
The only kind that you enjoy,
The recognition of a limitation
On idiosyncrasy, a choice
That, being narrow, can be seen as free.'

Thus your first fairy godmother, I suppose,
A learned, solemn, even a pedantic lady,
Edwardian resident of Bruges and Rome
Where she pursues her out-of-date researches
Into 'The Natural History' (save the mark)
'Of Genius'. Now I hear her sister,
The junior counsel but the cleverer,
Though in the plural, yet in other terms, address you
Not altogether to the same effect:

'The benefits that are at my discretion are
Particularizings of the general scope
This lady has endowed you with; and first,
Although a flair is of another order
Than what we give, yet as no spectacle
Is more to be pitied than of one who has
The genius, or to speak more properly
The temperament, and no aptitude, we give
Inalienable technical command.

Then, for your freedom: it is absolute.
Your law unto yourself is absolute
That you be lawless. Since you have no choice
(My colleague's paradox) you have
Absolute choice. Exceptionally fated
To break all rules, you are to find the rules
Of art and conduct waived. The moral law
Lapses before the selfless man, possessed
Of no one self, but of and by a style.'

'Not that you have,' the first impetuously
Resuming cried, 'no duty to be pure . . .'
'In heart', I fear she would have said; but here
The modern muse broke in on her with 'Pure,
Purged of all bearings on a human need,
The truest poem's at most a golden standish,
A tray to put your pens in.' Then a murmur
That swelled beneath the voices broke
Into a shout excluding all the muses.

It was the chorus of the acclamation lately
Accorded you as legendary hero,
Dilating on your prodigality,
Your arrogance, your abandonment, your art,
Though that seemed incidental. In the din
I caught by starts the sisters crying still,
And once the elder sounded menacing:
'Some have enjoyed what here I deny to you,
A self-betrayal not betrayed in art.'

The Mushroom Gatherers

AFTER MICKIEWICZ

Strange walkers! See their processional
Perambulations under low boughs,
The birches white, and the green turf under.
These should be ghosts by moonlight wandering.

Their attitudes strange: the human tree
Slowly revolves on its bole. All around
Downcast looks; and the direct dreamer
Treads out in trance his lane, unwavering.

Strange decorum: so prodigal of bows,
Yet lost in thought and self-absorbed, they meet
Impassively, without acknowledgment.
A courteous nation, but unsociable.

Field full of folk, in their immunity
From human ills, crestfallen and serene.
Who would have thought these shades our lively friends?
Surely these acres are Elysian Fields.

England

The Wind at Penistone

The wind meets me at Penistone.
                            A hill
Curves empty through the township, on a slope
Not cruel, and yet steep enough to be,
Were it protracted, cruel.
                            In the street,
A plain-ness rather meagre than severe,
Affords, though quite unclassical, a vista
So bald as to be monumental.
                                    Here
A lean young housewife meets me with the glance
I like to think that I can recognize
As dour, not cross.
                        And all the while the wind,
A royal catspaw, toying easily,
Flicks out of shadows from a tufted wrist,
Its mane, perhaps, this lemon-coloured sun.

The wind reserves, the hill reserves, the style
Of building houses on the hill reserves
A latent edge;
                    which we can do without
In Pennine gradients and the Pennine wind,
And never miss, or, missing it, applaud
The absence of the aquiline;
                                    which in her
Whose style of living in the wind reserves
An edge to meet the wind's edge, we may miss
But without prejudice.
                            And yet in art
Where all is patent, and a latency
Is manifest or nothing, even I,
Liking to think I feel these sympathies,
Can hardly praise this clenched and muffled style.

For architecture asks a cleaner edge,
Is open-handed.
                    And close-fisted people
Are mostly vulgar; only in the best,
Who draw, inflexible, upon reserves,
Is there a stern game that they play with life,
In which the rule is not to show one's hand
Until compelled.
                    And then the lion's paw!
Art that is dour and leonine in the Alps
Grows kittenish, makes curios and clocks,
Giant at play.
                    Here, nothing. So the wind
Meets me at Penistone, and, coming home,
The poet falls to special pleading, chilled
To find in Art no fellow but the wind.

Under St Paul's

Wren and Barry, Rennie and Mylne and Dance
    Under the flags, the men who stood for stone
    Lie in the stone. Carillons, pigeons once
Sluiced Ludgate's issues daily, and the dome
    Of stone-revetted crystal swung and hung
    Its wealth of waters. Wren had plugged it home
With a crypt at the nerve of London. Now the gull
    Circles the dry stone nozzles of the belfries,
    Each graceful City hydrant of the full
Eagerly brimming measure of agreement,
    Still to be tapped by any well-disposed
    Conversible man, still underneath the pavement
Purling and running, affable and in earnest,
    The conduit, Candour. Fattily urbane
    Under the great drum, pigeons foul their nest.

The whiter wing, Anger, and the gull's
Shearwater raucous over hunting hulls
Seek London's river. Rivers underground,
Under the crypt, return the sound

Of footfalls in the evening city. Out of wells,
Churchyards sunk behind Fleet Street, trickle smells
Of water where a calm conviction spoke
Now dank and standing. Leaves and our debris choke
The bell-note Candour that the pavior heard
Fluting and swelling like a crop-filled bird.

So sound the tides of love; yet man and woman
    May be my world's first movers, and the stream
    Still run no darker nowhere deeper than
Conviction's claim upon us, to deny
    Nothing that's undeniable. Light airs
    Are bent to the birds that couple as they fly
And slide and soar, yet answer to the flow
    Of this broad water under. There we ride
    Lent to the current, and convictions grow
In those they are meant for. As conviction's face
    Is darker than the speculative air,
    So and no darker is the place
For candour and love. What fowl lives underwater,
    Breeds in that dark? And hadn't a contriver
    Of alphabets, Cadmus, the gull for daughter?

Across the dark face of the waters
Flies the white bird. And the waters
Mount, mount, or should mount; we grow surer
Of what we know, if no surer
Of what we think. For on ageing
Labouring now and subsiding and nerveless wing
The gull sips the body of water, and the air
Packed at that level can hold up a minster in air.
Across the dark face of the water
Flies the white bird until nothing is left but the water.

Derbyshire Turf

That, true to the contours which round it
    Out and lie close,
The best beauty is barbarous, grounded
    On foreign bodies,
Flush to their angles, ungainly,
    Pawkily true –
Derbyshire turf, you tried vainly
    To point such a moral
When we, in our warmly remembered
    Youth, from the old
Armstrong Siddeley tourer descended
    Shouting upon you.

Then as now it was just where the boulder
    Lay scantily buried,
Or the gritstone poked up a shoulder,
    You sported your streaks
Of a specially sumptuous darkened
    Lush olive green –
Yet in those days none of us hearkened
    To this intimation
That where most intriguingly mounded
    Abrupt in its curves,
Beauty is richest and rounded
    Home on the truth.

Very well. Still we should wonder
    As farmers who loaded
Wagons with stones to lay under
    The grass of their pastures.
Much the same is the poet who prizing
    The shape of the truth
Studies to find some surprising
    Eccentric perception
To validate memory. Boys
    Are willing to guess
At the rock which lies under their joy's
    Elusiveness.

Dissentient Voice

When some were happy as the grass was green,
I was as happy as a glass was dark,
Chill eye beneath the chapel floor unseen
Most of the year, a mystery, the Ark.

Aboveboard rose the largely ethical
Glossy-with-graining pulpit; underground
The older Scriptures trembled for the Fall
And lapped at Adam with a sucking sound.

Grass-rooted goodness and a joy unmixed
Parch unbaptized inside a droughty head;
Arcadia's floor is not so firmly fixed
But it must tremble to a pastor's tread.

2. DISSENT. A FABLE

When Bradbury sang, 'The Roast Beef of Old England'
And Watts, 'How doth the little busy bee',
Then Doddridge blessed the pikes of Cumberland
And plunging sapphics damned eternally.

Said Watts the fox: 'Your red meat is uncouth.
We'll keep the bleeding purchase out of sight.
Arminian honey for the age's tooth!
With so much sweetness, who will ask for light?'

Wolf Bradbury mauled the synod, but the fox
Declared that men were growing more refined;
And honey greased, where blood would rust, the locks
That clicked when Calvin trapped the open mind.

The wolves threw off sheeps' clothing once or twice
(For Queen Anne dead, or the Pretender foiled).
But the fox knew that tastes were growing nice
And unction kept the hinge of dogma oiled.

Foxes however are their own worst foes;
And now their chapel door stands open wide,
Its hinge so clogged with wax it cannot close,
No fish so queer but he can swim inside.

The queerest fishes hunger for the trap
And wish the door would close on them, the rough
Jaws of Geneva and Old England snap:
They think their church not barbarous enough.

The fable seems extravagant, no doubt.
But Reynard ruled the roosts of heaven then,
And beastly pastors kept true shepherds out
While pike and barracuda fished for men.

3. PORTRAIT OF THE ARTIST AS A FARMYARD FOWL

Pluming himself upon a sense of sin
    (Lice in his feathers' undersides)
He sported drab, the sooner Faith to win.
    Old zealots were such sobersides;
He felt their gooseflesh crawl upon his skin
    And hoped to feel their zeal besides.

Since then this would-be puritan has paced
    A cock unmatched although so spurred;
Purist who crowed at shadows, he debased
    The rate of evil and conferred
Its rights on squalor, out of sheer good taste.
    No hag would ride on such a bird.

Dark plumes, though puritanical in cut,
    Still clothe the cock of the studied walk;
A conscious carriage must become a strut;
    Fastidiousness can only stalk
And seem at last not even tasteful but
    A ruffled hen too apt to squawk.

4. A GATHERED CHURCH

In memoriam A.E.D. ob. 1939
Deacon, you are to recognize in this
The idlest of my avocations, fruit
Of some late casual studies and my need
(Not dire, nor much acknowledged as a claim
Upon your known munificence) for what
You as lay preacher loved and disavowed,
The mellow tang of eloquence – a food
I have some skill in rendering down from words
Suppose them choice and well matured. I heard
Such from your bee-mouth once. A tarnished sun
Swirling the motes which swarmed along its shaft
Mixed soot with spices, and with honey, dust;
And memories of that winning unction now
Must countenance this application. For
I see them tumbled in a frowzy beam,
The grains of dust or pollen from our past,
Our common stock in family and church,
Asking articulation. These affairs
Touched you no doubt more nearly; you are loath
To see them made a gaud of rhetoric. But, sir,
I will deal plainly with you. They are past,
Past hoping for as you had hoped for them
For sixty years or more the day you died,
And if I seem a fribble in this case
No matter. For I will be eloquent
And on these topics, having little choice.

You who were once an orator should know
How these things are decided, not by chance
Although to think so is our best recourse;
For we may pledge our faith that they are solved
In part by fervent feeling and in part
By strenuous intellection – so they are,
But by all these under the guise of chance,
Of happy yet exacting accident,
Out of whose bounty suddenly a word
Of no apparent pertinence or force
Will promise unaccountably to draw
The whole lax beam into a burning glass.

So here I take the husk of my research,
A form of words – the phrase, 'a gathered church',
A rallying cry of our communions once
For you perhaps still stirring, but for me
A picturesque locution, nothing more
Except for what it promises, a tang.
Here is the promise of the burning-glass;
Now turn it in the variegated light.

'A gathered church.' That posy, the elect,
Was gathered in, not into, garden-walls;
For God must out of sheer caprice resect
The jugular stalks of those He culls and calls.

Watts thought his church, though scant of privilege,
Walled in its own communion. In its walks
Some may have doubted if so sparse a hedge
Tempered the blast to blooms still on their stalks.

It was the rooted flower could be hurt:
The plucked that lived in living water felt
No more the stress of time, the tug of dirt.
Time lost for good the fragrance Heaven smelt.

When blossoms crowd into the waist of time,
Those cut and chosen for the eternal vase
Rot down to no kind humus, rather climb
And spend their charity upon the stars.

Abundant friction: not a deal of heat.
These are, you know, preliminary rites,
A form of invocation. So the glass
Is moved and dances, waterish, flashes out
Now on the wall, now on the floor . . . But now
Your face swims up athwart the light,
The silken, heavy, iron-grey moustache
That reaffirms conciliatory smiles
Dispensing honey with a Dorset burr;
The hollow temples of a young man's brow;
The mild and beaming eye; the cheek still apple-hale.
Appealing gestures pregnantly curtailed

49

Conveyed impulsive courtesies, refined
The gross freak of your corpulence. That head
Was bowed beneath reproaches mostly mute
When 'Charity begins at home,' we said,
Feeling the pinch of your more public alms
Wise in our generations. And indeed
You thought so too; your home was somewhere else
And there you ran most fruitfully to seed.
Now all the churches gathered from the world
Through that most crucial bottleneck of Grace,
That more than hourglass, being waspish, waist
Where all the flutes of love are gathered in,
The girdle of Eternity, the strait
Too straitened for the sands and sons of Time,
More mean and private than the sticking-place
Of any partial loyalties – all these
In you, dear sir, are justified. Largesse,
Suppose it but of rhetoric, endears,
Disseminated quite at large to bless
The waste, superb profusion of the spheres.

Ireland

The Priory of St Saviour, Glendalough

A carving on the jamb of an embrasure,
'Two birds affronted with a human head
Between their beaks' is said to be
'Uncertain in its significance but
A widely known design.' I'm not surprised.

For the guidebook cheats: the green road it advises
In fact misled; and a ring of trees
Screened in the end the level knoll on which
St Saviour's, like a ruin on a raft,
Surged through the silence.

I burst through brambles, apprehensively
Crossed an enormous meadow. I was there.
Could holy ground be such a foreign place?
I climbed the wall, and shivered. There flew out
Two birds affronted by my human face.

Samuel Beckett's Dublin

When it is cold it stinks, and not till then.
The seasonable or more rabid heats
Of love and summer in some other cities
Unseal the all too human: not in his.
When it is cold it stinks, but not before;

Smells to high heaven then most creaturely
When it is cold. It stinks, but not before
His freezing eye has done its best to maim,
To amputate limbs, livelihood and name,
Abstracting life beyond all likelihood.

When it is cold it stinks, and not till then
Can it be fragrant. On canal and street,
Colder and colder, Murphy to Molloy,
The weather hardens round the Idiot Boy,
The gleeful hero of the long retreat.

When he is cold he stinks, but not before,
This living corpse. The existential weather
Smells out in these abortive minims, men
Who barely living therefore altogether
Live till they die; and sweetly smell till then.

North Dublin

St George's, Hardwicke Street,
Is charming in the Church of Ireland fashion:
The best of Geneva, the best of Lambeth
Aesthetically speaking
In its sumptuously sober
Interior, meet.

A continuous gallery, clear glass in the windows
An elegant conventicle
In the Ionian order –
What dissenter with taste
But would turn, on these terms
Episcopalian?

'Dissenter' and 'tasteful' are contradictions
In terms, perhaps, and my fathers
Would ride again to the Boyne
Or with scythes to Sedgemoor, or splinter
The charming fanlights in this charming slum
By their lights, rightly.

Corrib. An Emblem

Hairless and worse than leathery, the skin
Of the great ogre, Connemara, mounded
Silvery, fathoms thick. Within
The crook of tutelary arm that cradled
The Corrib's urn, the subcutaneous waters
In their still blue as bright as blood shone out,
By healed-up puckers where his pre-divinity
Was scored and trenched. To him suppose a Daphne
Pursued by art Palladian, picturesque,
Or else Hispanic through the Galway Lynches,
Merchant adventurers turning Medici,
Virtù in freight. Underneath his shoulder
Syrinx, the villa seen across the lough,
A reed now broken, flourished. In his hand
A nymph took root, and here and there a laurel.

The Wearing of the Green

Gold is not autumn's privilege;
A tawny ripening
In Meath in May burns ready in the hedge;
The yellow that will follow spring
Accentuates its wet and green array,
A sumptuous trill beneath
The shriller edge
Of Meath in May.

Green more entire must needs be evergreen,
Precluding autumn and this spring
Of Meath in May, its in-between
Of golds and yellows preluding
The liquid summer. Must the seasons stay
Their temperate career because
A flag is green
In Meath in May?

Imagination, Irish avatar,
Aches in the spring's heart and in mine, the stranger's,
In Meath in May. But to believe there are
Unchanging Springs endangers,
By that fast dye, the earth;
So blood-red green the season,
It never changes
In Meath in May.

Italy

Going to Italy

Though painters say Italian light does well
By natural features and by monuments,
Our eyes may not be fine enough to tell
Effects compounded of such elements.

And yet we trust our judgment as to fires
In their effects more subtle still, like love,
Which is a light that dwells about its squires
To tell the world what they are thinking of.

That fortunate climate is so apt for this,
As some aver, that not a thought can pass
Through spiritual natures, but it is
Seen in the air, like glitter in a glass.

If Rome should see us bathed in such a flue,
And all our even inward motions edged
Thus with the crispness of their follow-through,
I'd think not we but Rome was privileged.

Tuscan Morning

Presences are always said to brood;
And in the Boboli gardens just at noon
Toad-like Silenus squats inside a shade
While Michelangelo's giants cannot break
The curtain of their element, the haze.

But this is hardly Italy. At least
This is in Italy the hour and the place
That throw our Italy into high relief,
Which is italic cursive and alert
In early mornings and late afternoons.

High noon of the Renaissance was in Rome
This was the Tuscan, Brunelleschi's morning,
The guidebooks say. What have renaissances
To do with noon? It is the edge of light
Goes cleaving, windless presence, like a ray.

Mr Sharp in Florence

'Mr Sharp from Sheffield, straight out of the knifebox.'

Americans are innocents abroad;
But Sharp from Sheffield is the cagey kind
And – out of the knifebox, bleeding – can't afford
To bring to Florence such an open mind.

Poor Mr Sharp! And happy transatlantic
Travellers, so ingenuous! But some
Are so alert they can finesse the trick,
So strong they know when to be overcome.

Now must he always fall between these stools?
Blind, being keen; dumb, so as not to shrill;
Grounded and ground in logic-chopping schools;
So apt in so inapposite a skill?

Beleaguered and unsleeping sentinel,
He learned the trick of it, before the end;
Saw a shape move, and could not see it well,
Yet did not challenge, but himself cried, 'Friend!'

Via Portello

'Nobody wants any more poems about . . . foreign cities.'
MR KINGSLEY AMIS

Rococo compositions of decay,
Each a still-life, the fruity garbage-heaps
Teem by themselves. A broad and cobbled way,

Tiepolo's and Byron's thoroughfare
Lies grand and empty in its sullied air,
And watches while the rest of Padua sleeps.

The conscious vista closed at either end,
Here by a palace, that way by a gate
At night pure Piranesi . . . Yes, my friend,
I know you have decided for your part
That poems on foreign cities and their art
Are the privileged classes' shorthand. You must wait;

Or, traversing the colonnaded mile
Of this decayed locality, extend
The warmth of your resentment to the style
Of Padua's poor. A civilisation broken
Around them, theirs; and want, and no word spoken –
The conscious vista closed at either end.

The Tuscan Brutus

The Duke insists you stay; you could do worse.
You temporize, and promise him a fine
Head for his medal. As for the reverse,
That (now he jests) Lorenzo shall design.

That melancholy madman Lorenzino
De Medici, in sole attendance there,
Takes up the joke, agrees. The Duke should know
The risk he's running, but that's his affair.

There's more to this than meets your knowing eye,
Cellini, though we owe the tale to you:
You made one, but he made another die;
You were to strike the medal – he struck too.

He writes that his design is under way,
Claims that its greatness will be manifest
To later ages, and that night and day
He thinks of nothing else, and cannot rest.

A sad reverse it proved. Were you to know
Your lovely art had such a seamy side?
Amazed, you saw the spun coin fall to show
The antique motif of tyrannicide.

No end of tyrants – after Alessandro
Duke Cosimo . . . Oh you were right, of course:
For current coin his style would never do.
Yet for a medal yours was rather coarse.

The Pacer in the Fresco. John the Baptist

Already running, sprang from the womb; met,
Adored, inclined to, passed the Overtaker;
Fore-ran Him then around the course; and yet
Drew Him abreast, baptized Him into the lead
He need not challenge for – then in a stride
Took up the killing pace, and shook a bead
Of cool sweat on the Runner by his side.

Met from the first none could be waited for:
His father with a minatory gesture
Full of a blessing was fulfilled before
Much like a curse; his mother then, resigned,
Delivered still delivering – from whom
Departing running, he is first to find
The stadium packed and roaring with their doom.

Turns the last corner, round into the straight,
Into the last fierce panels of the fresco
Indomitably, the Pursuer's gait
Steady behind him and the easy breath
Fanning his cheek. He can afford to fall
Out of the running, when he sees his death,
Beating a foot, dance out along the wall;

Sees perjured judges clap the Victor in
After a lonelier circuit, and the headsman
Timekeeper plunge the stopwatch and begin

The ritual decollation of the flag
Ripe for its fall; and sees, at his command,
The pear-shaped classical canon start to sag
And sway down ripe, his ripeness come to hand.

We went to gape. But when the unflurried Athlete
Hove up behind, with high unhurried action,
Running so well within himself, His feet
Firm on the track, not flying, no one's eye
But left the lunging leader, though in profile
So aquiline, or knew him going by
Except as promise of a purer style.

The two-dimensional hero, moving fast,
Himself the movement, like the knife-edge angel
Of all annunciations, couldn't last:
He clove too cleanly ever to belong
In the close composition of a whole,
Himself too much the equilibrist for long
To tilt a saucer on the wading soul.

The Fountain

Feathers up fast, and steeples; then in clods
Thuds into its first basin; thence as surf
Smokes up and hangs; irregularly slops
Into its second, tattered like a shawl;
There, chill as rain, stipples a danker green,
Where urgent tritons lob their heavy jets.

For Berkeley this was human thought, that mounts
From bland assumptions to inquiring skies,
There glints with wit, fumes into fancies, plays
With its negations, and at last descends,
As by a law of nature, to its bowl
Of thus enlightened but still common sense.

We who have no such confidence must gaze
With all the more affection on these forms,
These spires, these plumes, these calm reflections, these
Similitudes of surf and turf and shawl,
Graceful returns upon acceptances.
We ask of fountains only that they play,

Though that was not what Berkeley meant at all.

Chrysanthemums

Chrysanthemums become a cult because
No Japanese interior is snug;
For even Fuji can be brought indoors
As lamps turn amber in an opal fog.

Here in the thick of opals, where the horn
Blurts from the seaward mountain through the pall,
Now fires are lit and the snug curtains drawn,
Shock-headed clusters warm the dripping wall.

A brazier or the perforated tin
Of watchmen huddled at a dockyard gate
Glows with such amber as the night draws in
As these bronze flowers, blossoming so late.

Chrysanthemum, cult of the Japanese,
You teach me no Penates can be lost
While men can draw together as they freeze
And make a domesticity of frost.

Yet bivouacs of Revolution throw
Threatening shadows and a scorching heat;
And embers of unequal summer glow
A hearth indeed, but in a looted street.

Cherry Ripe

On a Painting by Juan Gris

No ripening curve can be allowed to sag
On cubist's canvas or in sculptor's stone:
Informal fruit, that burgeons from the swag,
Would spoil the ripening that is art's alone.

This can be done with cherries. Other fruit
Have too much bloom of import, like the grape,
Whose opulence comes welling from a root
Struck far too deep to yield so pure a shape.

And Cherry ripe, indeed ripe, ripe, I cry.
Let orchards flourish in the poet's soul
And bear their feelings that are mastered by
Maturing rhythms, to compose a whole.

But how the shameful grapes and olives swell,
Excrescent from no cornucopia, tart,
Too near to oozing to be handled well:
Ripe, ripe, they cry, and perish in my heart.

Hearing Russian Spoken

Unsettled again and hearing Russian spoken
I think of brokenness perversely planned
By Dostoievsky's debauchees; recall
The 'visible brokenness' that is the token
Of the true believer; and connect it all
With speaking a language I cannot command.

If broken means unmusical I speak
Even in English brokenly, a man
Wretched enough, yet one who cannot borrow
Their hunger for indignity nor, weak,
Abet my weakness, drink to drown a sorrow
Or write in metres that I cannot scan.

Unsettled again at hearing Russian spoken,
'Abjure politic brokenness for good',
I tell myself. 'Recall what menaces,
What self-loathings must be re-awoken:
This girl and that, and all your promises
Your pidgin that they too well understood.'

Not just in Russian but in any tongue
Abandonment, morality's soubrette
Of lyrical surrender and excess,
Knows the weak endings equal to the strong;
She trades on broken English with success
And, disenchanted, I'm enamoured yet.

Limited Achievement

(Piranesi, *Prisons*, Plate VI)

Seeing his stale vocabulary build
The same décor – observe this 'gloomy vault' –
We tire of this good fellow, highly skilled
No doubt, but pertinacious to a fault.

The same few dismal properties, the same
Oppressive air of justified unease,
Proclaim the practised hand from which they came,
Although these show a willingness to please.

Yes, some attempt undoubtedly was made
To lift the composition, and to pierce
The bald tympana – vainly, I'm afraid;
The effect remains, as ever, gaunt and fierce.

Those were his true proclivities? Perhaps.
Successful in his single narrow track,
He branches out, but only to collapse,
Imprisoned in his own unhappy knack,

Which, when unfailing, fails him most, perhaps.

A Winter Talent

Lighting a spill late in the afternoon,
I am that coal whose heat it should unfix;
Winter is come again, and none too soon
For meditation on its raft of sticks.

Some quick bright talents can dispense with coals
And burn their boats continually, command
An unreflecting brightness that unrolls
Out of whatever firings come to hand.

What though less sunny spirits never turn
The dry detritus of an August hill
To dangerous glory? Better still to burn
Upon that gloom where all have felt a chill.

Under a Skylight

Through a wide window all Somerset might look in
At the quiet act of love, but where we lie
Under a skylight in a double bed,
I cannot ignore the scrutinizing sky
Night's Peeping Tom. Could anyone turn his head,
However coarse in fibre, to begin
(With that mild aperture so wide above)
The tumultuous quiet of the act of love?

Skylight, that's heaven's light: an easy clue
For prurient exegetes supposing shame
Brazen on earth less bold in heaven's eye.
But down the dim shaft those slanted timbers frame,
Our four eyes glitter upwards at the sky
Like pussies in a well; and we pursue
Untouched by shame a feline interest
Compulsively, at nobody's behest.

No. Let's hear nothing of those notorious twins
Identical but different, Agape
And Eros, whom the mind
Like a celibate uncle pats uncertainly;
It puzzles me the more, though, why I find
An image for the married state that wins
My uncommitted heart, in these wide-eyed
Unsleeping bodies gazing side by side.

Gardens no Emblems

Man with a scythe: the torrent of his swing
Finds its own level; and is not hauled back
But gathers fluently, like water rising
Behind the watergates that close a lock.

The gardener eased his foot into a boot;
Which action like the mower's had its mould,
Being itself a sort of taking root,
Feeling for lodgment in the leather's fold.

But forms of thought move in another plane
Whose matrices no natural forms afford
Unless subjected to prodigious strain:
Say, light proceeding edgewise, like a sword.

The Nonconformist

X, whom society's most mild command,
For instance evening dress, infuriates,
In art is seen confusingly to stand
For disciplined conformity, with Yeats.

Taxed to explain what this resentment is
He feels for small proprieties, it comes,
He likes to think, from old enormities
And keeps the faith with famous martyrdoms.

Yet it is likely, if indeed the crimes
His fathers suffered rankle in his blood,
That he finds least excusable the times
When they acceded, not when they withstood.

How else explain this bloody-minded bent
To kick against the prickings of the norm;
When to conform is easy, to dissent;
And when it is most difficult, conform?

Rejoinder to a Critic

You may be right: 'How can I dare to feel?'
May be the only question I can pose,
'And haply by abstruse research to steal
From my own nature all the natural man'
My sole resource. And I do not suppose
That others may not have a better plan.

And yet I'll quote again, and gloss it too
(You know by now my liking for collage):
Donne could be daring, but he never knew,
When he inquired, 'Who's injured by my love?'
Love's radio-active fall-out on a large
Expanse around the point it bursts above.

'Alas, alas, who's injured by my love?'
And recent history answers: Half Japan!
Not love, but hate? Well, both are versions of
The 'feeling' that you dare me to . . . Be dumb!
Appear concerned only to make it scan!
How dare we now be anything but numb?

Heigh-ho on a Winter Afternoon

There is a heigh-ho in these glowing coals
By which I sit wrapped in my overcoat
As if for a portrait by Whistler. And there is
A heigh-ho in the bird that noiselessly
Flew just now past my window, to alight
On winter's moulding, snow; and an alas,
A heigh-ho and a desultory chip,
Chip, chip on stone from somewhere down below.

Yes I have 'mellowed', as you said I would,
And that's a heigh-ho too for any man;
Heigh-ho that means we fall short of alas
Which sprigs the grave of higher hopes than ours.
Yet heigh-ho too has its own luxuries,
And salts with courage to be jocular
Disreputable sweets of wistfulness,
By deprecation made presentable.

What should we do to rate the long alas
But skeeter down a steeper gradient?
And then some falls are still more fortunate,
The meteors spent, the tragic heroes stunned
Who go out like a light. But here the chip,
Chip, chip will flake the stone by slow degrees,
For hour on hour the fire will gutter down,
The bird will call at longer intervals.

Poems of 1955–6

On Sutton Strand

I saw brown Corrib lean upon his urn,
 And shawled Andromeda by the Atlantic sea;
I thought smooth eastern provinces would turn
 To emblems of an equal suavity;
I thought that, nearer by a hundred miles
To Europe's heart, the Mediterranean styles
 And milder forms of nature would agree.

But fables worked by what was fabulous.
 It is the mildest proves intractable.
And here it is the sky that silences
 The flutes of Greece and Sicily with the full
Chime of its equability. The bright
Items of colour glitter in a light
 That makes men small and all their fables dull.

What in a seascape so entirely Dutch
 Can Orpheus do but just believe his eyes?
No more the broad brush and the master's touch;
 He has no choice now but to itemize
Bright fleck by fleck, and try by being neat
Where to command is hopeless, to compete
 With an indifference equal to the sky's.

Aubade

I wish for you that when you wake
You emulate the leaf and bird;
That like them, touched with grace, you take
Note of the wind. You have not heard
Its low-voiced billows yet, nor seen
(Lost in your less elated rest)
The empty light upon the green,
The leaves and tumbling birds that gave
The wind its due, and then redressed
That small excess, each bounding spray
A boat that dances on the wave,
A whip that tingles in the day.

69

Dudwood

The roads getting emptier, air in a steadily purer
Stream flowing back past the old Armstrong Siddeley tourer;
Then, the next morning, at large in the boulderstrewn
    woodland –
What worlds away from our nest in the chimney of England!
The turf carpets laid for us, scroll-like or star-shaped or trefoiled,
Deep pile to the tread of the spring-heel Jack Sparrows of
    Sheffield.

The bluff before Birchover, fronting the valley and shaded
By rowan and pine where the outcrop capped the precipitous
Comber of meadow. That way, in search of Cos lettuce
Or pony-tailed carrots, the three of us often ascended
That very first morning – all ardent and plumed, all cockaded
With springing abandonments, lost now, barely remembered.

Dublin Georgian

A room designed by Orrery receives
The Roscius of the hour.
He bows and smiles and pauses by the door
Among less battered *putti*; but perceives
Advance towards him, borne upon a sea
Of smoke and noise,
The lady of a rival company
Whose progress West, the stuccodore, convoys
With birds and flutes. Now mutually entreating
By signs, they draw together; and one sees,
As exclamations punctuate their meeting,
The crisp swags droop a little on the frieze.

Were I to move among the talkers here,
I'd soon be disabused
About this artist, hearing him traduced
Wherever laughing malice has the ear
Of Irish wit. But I avert my gaze,
Refuse to know

His marxist and his mystagogic phase,
Or the connubial scandal years ago
Retailed around me. Every Irish master
Must learn to suffer, for the nation's sake,
The national proclivity for plaster,
Mouldings that chip, and pediments that flake.

The author of the genial comedies
From which this pair plucked fruit,
The edible stucco of their shared repute,
Has made no entrance; and yet there he is,
A brow that's broader than the marble mantel
There in the wall
Which thin heads nod in front of. Broad as well
Behind the brow, the soul. Broadness of soul –
What an inelegant and Russian notion!
It's more than Orrery could cater for.
His walls distend, the cornice is in motion . . .
Oliver Goldsmith! Samson heaves the floor.

Dublin Georgian (2)

A thin brown orphan in his washed-out blue
Opens the door a crack
Behind its sunblind and, subdued, peers through
At the wrecked street behind us. Standing back
He lets us into elegance preserved,
As he is, from the slum;
This orphanage, number twenty, that has served
Him as asylum, harbours also some
Few sedulous fragilities refined
On wall and ceiling. As we follow him
Beneath the famous plasterwork, I find
Art too (thus orphaned) vulnerably slim.

In rapt obscenities, the instructed taste
Admires the moulding, sighs
'Ah' at the staircase, and extols the chaste
Ceilings by Stapleton; occupies

(Thin shoulders raised, a flutter of bony hands)
The pure *gestalt*
Of the double arch; expatiates, understands
How architect and plasterer had felt
The underpinning of that virile beauty
In an age's order. Later, in the street,
He held forth to me how the artist's duty
Is mutiny, evasion, and retreat.

Eden

Adam had found what was not his to seek,
Command of motives; and the world grew heated,
The self extended and the will elated.
He can, he sees, make Eve again attractive
Almost at will, using this new technique
For rousing, as for quenching, an incentive.

A sin in gardens, where the shadows' play
Makes clarity a sin. So the attendant
Shows them the door. The garden was abandoned
To twilight, seasons, and the steady tread
Of natural wants that, once met, fell away,
Chill in the evenings, gratefully exhausted.

The Waterfall at Powerscourt

Looping off feline through the leisured air
    Water, a creature not at home in water,
Takes to the air. It comes down on its forepaws, changes
    Feet on the rockface and again extended
Bounds.   For it neither
    Pours nor is poured, but only here on its quarry
Falls at last, pours. No more the amphibious otter
    Than foundered ram can walk this water thrown
Catwalk across a further element.

Water itself is not at home in water
    But fails its creatures, as a fallen nature
Swerves from its course. And, less adaptable,
    Out of an element itself thrown out
The fallen creature cannot find itself
    Nor its own level, headlong.

Or else as a sealion, heavy and limber,
    Sedately slithers its short rock chute in the zoo
(Foolish and haughty as, propped on a stock, the Prince Regent),
    And over the water it takes to
Shoots,   so the water
    Lobs itself, immerses in rock and, rebounding,
Surfaces smoothly backwards into space,
    Swimming the air as for freshwater miles offshore
The Orinoco dyes the ocean cold.

What end it answers, over the Sabine country
    Of Mrs Rafferty's Tusculum and Dublin's
Weekend hinterland, arching; or what use
    Insinuating underneath that ocean
Its chill of wit, who knows? The end it answers,
    The level it seeks, is its own.

from *The Forests of Lithuania* (1959)

'White walls shone from far'

White walls shone from far
White against green of poplars'
Windbreak against Autumn.
The house no great one, but the barn
Great, and with stacks beside it,
Gross country, full with foison.
Enter to these the youth
Beneath ancestral portraits,
Ancestral, and of heroes:
Kosciusko sworn and sworded
To drive three powers from Poland
Or fall upon that sword;
Rejtan, a Life of Cato
And the Phaedo before him,
These, and a knife turned inward;
Jasinski smiting the Russians
With Korsak, on the ravelin
Of Praga burning behind them.
Enter to these Tadeusz,
And to the grandfather clock
That plays Dombrowski's march,
And to his room when a boy . . .

'The Lithuanian Judge'

The Lithuanian judge
Offers by way of reproof
To the young Pan Tadeusz
Decorum, the difficult science,
No matter of graceful posture
Or ease at the affable counter,
But bearing of old Poland;
Courtesy, being extended
To all, not without distinction
But in the mode most proper
As to master with man, or to children
With parents, or each to each

In public husband and wife.
'Discourse in noble mansions
Was then a persistent history,
And talk among the gentry
The annals of their provinces;
Gentlemen watched their step,
Knowing such pains were taken
To judge of their deserving.
But neither name nor stock,
Associates nor achievements
Are now enquired after,
And each goes where he pleases
Short of the known informer
And the scrounger by profession.
Vespasian never questioned
Out of what hands his riches
Came to him, having decided
Money was "not to be sniffed at".
So men approve a title
By current estimates,
As if to strike up a friendship
Were also a transaction.
But a sense of personal worth
Is arrived at only by weighing;
The beam is only plumb
With a counterpoise in the pan,
A worthiness in another.'

'And so to the Legions!'

And so to the legions!
So to news of the legions!
And yet not here, not now.
Who swam across the Niemen?
Gorécki, Pac, and Obúchowitz,
Piotrówski and the Mirzejéwskis,
Brochócki and the Bernatówicz brothers,
Not here, not now. Perhaps
Later in private Robak

The Bernadine, the almoner
Of a foreign house, his bearing
So soldierly (and a sabre's
Cut on the brow), will take
A knife to scapulary. Now
Talk of the coursing, talk
Of the old dispute with the Count
With a foible for the Gothick
Who wants our ruined castle . . .
Tomorrow the folk may read
Their own gazette's citations
In the bearing of their betters
With pride, or brokenly. Or else
An old maimed beggar stands
Having his crust; and then
Out with it – Dombrówski
Assembling on the plains
Of Lombardy; Kniázewicz
Among the captured eagles
In Rome; or Jablonówski,
His Danube Legion locked,
Among the sugar canes
And the pepper plants, with the blacks.

'Who does not remember his Boyhood'

Who does not remember his boyhood, gun on shoulder,
    Whistling through unobstructed fields?
Overstepping the bounds, yet offending no leaseholder
    Of Lithuania, where the chase was free?

There ocean-goer, unmarked ship, the hunter
    Ranged at large; as augur,
Read skies and clouds; or to townsmen occult, an enchanter,
    Heard the earth-whisper.

Look in vain for the landrail, as lost down the meadow calling
    As pike in the Niemen, and look
In vain overhead for the lark whose carillon falling
    Around us rings in the Spring.

There an eagle wing rustles, appalling the sparrows,
 A comet dismaying the stars. And a falcon,
Fluttering butterfly pinned, when a hare moves in the meadow
 Stoops like a meteor.

When will the Lord God have us return, inhabit
 Ancestral fields, bear arms
Against the birds, and only to ride down the rabbit
 Muster our horse?

'Telimena, the Lady of Fashion'

Telimena, the lady of fashion,
Installed in a summer villa
Outside St Petersburg:
When fate must send
To live next door
Dog-loving dull *chinovnik*,
Alarming dogs conspire to rend
The night, and drive her frantic.
Worse is in store:
The lady swoons
To see her spaniel mangled
By cruel beagles, and before
Her eyes abruptly strangled.
The culprits brought to book,
The Czar's own hunting-master
Bends his tremendous look
On hound and master. 'What,
You coursed a doe?' 'Milord,
It was a dog'. 'Indeed,
So you prevaricate?
The hunting laws of Muscovy
Are meant to be obeyed.'
Four weeks detention cures
Suburban householders
Of hunting out of season;
Their dogs endure a summary
Death, for the same good reason.

Thus Telimena
To the room at large,
Thus, with composure.
Who'd not condone
The dubious note
In such a lovely cause?
Triumph of tone!
Her anecdote
Draws laughter and applause.
And now the swain
Forgets the maid
To court this ampler fair
Who sets in train
The ambuscade
Of love, and baits the snare;
Now she delays
The murmured phrase
Which he must stoop to catch;
Her gaze his eyes,
His lips, her sighs
Mingle, and make the match.
Oh that a fly
Should come between
So close a tête-à-tête!
Pursuit, pass by
Nor intervene!
Domestic hygiene, wait!
Too late. The Seneschal
Has stalked his chosen fly
Too far. The blow must fall,
And fall it does. A start!
They jump apart,
Halves of a riven tree:
The lightning-stroke
Has cleft an oak
Of Love's own forestry.

The Forest

'O happy skies of Italy!
Rose gardens of the Caesars!'
'Classic cascades of Tibur,
And Posilippo's crag . . .'
Thus far that knight of the pencil,
The Count, and Telimena.

Yet round them even as they sigh
Lithuania's forests lie,
Currants wave their hop-crowned tresses,
Quickbeams blush like shepherdesses,
The hazel in a maenad's shape
Crowned with her nuts as with the grape
Twirls a green thyrsus, and below
The striplings of the forest grow –
The may, whom guelder-roses clip;
The blackberry, his ebon lip
Pressed to the raspberry's. Linking hands
(That's leaves) the trees and bushes stand
Like dancers, maid and man, around
The married pair in middle ground,
Two that for straightness, hue and height
Surpass their sylvan neighbours quite;
The silver birch, the well-loved bride,
Her man the hornbeam by her side.
Grave seniors sit some way apart
To watch their progeny disport,
Matronly poplar, hoary beech
Who gazing find no need of speech;
And a moss-bearded oak that bears
The weight of full five hundred years
Rests, as on tombstones overthrown,
On his own forebears turned to stone.

In the Botanical Garden at Wilno
Trees from eastward and southward
And trees of Italy grow,
And which of them all is preferred
Before our trees? Is the aloe

Its stem like a lightning rod
Their match? Or will they show
The lemon of the lacquered leaf,
Strung about with its wealth like a widow
Short and ill-favoured but moneyed?
Or is it that emblem of grief
(Of boredom, some would have said)
The long lean much belauded
Cypress, that over the dead
Like a German flunkey is set,
Not daring to stir his head
So strict the etiquette?

Blue, that Italian sky
Clear, as if frozen water;
But in this country
As the wind or the storm passes,
What images, what actions
The sportive wrack composes;
Shower-logged, sluggish in Spring
Clouds like tortoises labour
Over a sky where tresses
Of the long rain sway earthward;
The bowling hailstorm crosses
The heavens by balloon
Blue, but with yellow flashes;
And then, what metamorphoses
Pursue the white quotidian
Clouds that like a gaggle
Of swans or geese the falcon
Wind hard presses;
Harried, they multiply
Prodigies, and crested
With sudden manes as serried
Legs bud beneath them, coursers
Over the steppes of the sky,
Necks arched, they gallop.

★   ★   ★

Does the great oak, Baublis, survive
In whose age-scooped bulk

As in a stout house
Twelve sat at table? The grove
Of Mendog, does it bloom
Still by the churchyard wall?
And in the Ukraine does it rise
Still on the banks of the Ros,
That linden, pride
Of the Holowínskis, spreading
So wide its leaves
Before their house that a hundred
Young men have danced
Beneath, with a hundred maidens?

Monuments of our fathers!
How many among you yearly
Fall to contractors' axes?
Will such officious vandals
Unhouse all forest-warblers,
Bird or bard, to whom
Your shade was grateful? One,
The linden of Czarnólas,
Jan Kochanowski's descant,
Is singing still, and singing
Though to the bard of the Cossack
Of marvels still. And I,
A wretched shot, escaping
My comrades' gibes, how many
Fancies have I not taken,
A nobler game,
Out of your quiet! Bearded
Mosses around me silver,
The berries crushed and blue-ish
Streaked them, as the tussocks
Of heather reddened, strung
With the huckleberry's coral,
Rosaries. Around
Darkness lay as, low
Green clouds, the branches
Hung over me. Above
That stable vault,
The wind was somewhere wailing

Roaring or howling – odd
And stunning noise, as if
A sea suspended
Over my head swung, tossing.

Below, the remains of cities
Oak overthrown;
Breached wall and shattered column;
And branching stumps,
Beams half-powdered
In a hedge of grass.

Looking within is fearful:
Lords of the woods,
Wild boar and wolf
And bear, dwell here;
Unwary guest,
Bones half-gnawed at the entry.

A double column of water
Behind the green grass
Rises – a pair of antlers,
Stag; and a sunbeam falling
Athwart the trees
Extinguished, a beast passing.

And again, quiet.

Rapping on the fir-tree, woodpecker,
In flight, there . . .!
Lost. And the rapping
Starting again,
The hidden child
Needing to be sought for.

Squirrel, a nut in its forepaws,
Cuirassier crested
With its own tail,
Fearful although so armoured,
Darting its eyes;
It flies the intruder;

Tree to tree, a dancer,
Like lightning flashes;
Into a fissure
Unnoticed in a tree-stump
Sidles, returning
To tree-form this Dryad.

And again, quiet.

Who has plumbed Lithuania's forest,
Pressed to the thicket's core?
As the sea-floor is known to the fisherman
Meagrely, even inshore,
So the hunter can know of the forest
Only the face of its waters
Never their bed. Of its centre
What fable and rumour have said
Has authority. Once past
The manageable tangles,
The rampart rises – logs,
Roots, stumps, which a quagmire defends –
And water, and nets
Of rank weeds and ant-hills, and knots
Of snakes, and the wasp's and the hornet's
Nests. And then small meres
Grass-choked yet unplumbable, thought
To harbour devils, hold water
Rust-spotted, emitting a thick
And stinking steam. In the fumes
The trees are bald and sicken,
Dwarfed, wormlike; bare
Of bark and leaves, they wear beards
Of filthy fungi, and a knot
Of bunched-up mosses – witches
Around their pot, the pool,
Thawed by a graveplot brew.

These pools no eye can pass,
Still less a foot; morasses
Here raise, miasmal, shrouding
The further reaches, clouds

That rumour says obscure
From view a purer air
And fruitful earth, where all is
As in the ark. Metropolis
Of beasts and plants, the region
Sees brutes forget their rages
And learn civility. The seed
Of every plant that seeded
Throughout the earth is there
Preserved; and the primal pair
Of every creature copulates
In pre-lapsarian state.

Tradition will allow
The ancient buffalo
The bison and the bear
Alone the right to wear
The purple. All around,
Treed that they may command
The land's approaches, wait
Their ministers of state
The lynx and wolverine;
Beside them where they reign
Fed on their broken meats
The two court favourites
Eagle and falcon skulk;
Boar, wolf and antlered elk
Each in suburban fief
Owe vassalage. The chief
And patriarchal pairs
Stay home among their peers,
But send their progenies
Far out to colonize.

Themselves they know repose
Locked in their ancient ease
Never by cut or shot
To die, but of old age
In nature's course. They have
Likewise a place of graves
Wherein, when near to death,

Wildfowl bring home their feathers
And brutes their fur. The stag
Who barely moves his legs
Limps thither, and the bear
Who cannot chew, the hare
When his blood thickens, grey
Ravens and hawks that grow
Half-blind, and when cross-billed
So far as to withhold
The meat it craves, the old
Eagle. Inferior kinds
Whose bones no woodward finds
Within his walks, repair
When sick or hurt to expire
In that, their fatherland.

A polity well planned
Keeps order in the lair:
Meum nor *tuum* there
Embroil, and unaware
Of duelling or war
As once in Paradise
Keeping the peace, too wise
To butt or bite, the tame
And the wild consort. The same
Harmony would extend
Even to humankind;
Should ever human hunter
Although unarmed there enter,
Unhurt he'd pass between
The animals, and be seen
With that astonishment
Which their first fathers bent
On Adam when he first
Upon the sixth and last
Day of Creation ran
Through Eden. But to man
Death, Toil and Terror ban,
How luckily, access;
Nor can he ever press
To that secluded ground.

Only at times a hound
Fierce in pursuit may pass
Amid the pits and moss
And from what lies within
In terror run to whine,
Beneath his master's hand
Still quivering. Unscanned
By man, each ancient reach
Is called in hunter's speech
'Jungle'.

          Thou'dst little wit,
Bruin, in this haunt safe,
To venture out of it.
What didst so far from home?
Did ripe oats draw thee
Or the honeycomb
Along the open ride
Where trees grow sparsely
By the forest's side?
The ranger saw thee there
And sent his spies abroad
To learn from them the lair
Where thou o' nights hast slept
And where thou'st fed. And now
Thy foes have crept
To bar thee every road
Back to the jungle
And thine own abode.

The hunters strained their ears;
As to a curious discourse hearkening,
They heard the forest's silence
Play for them, where the dogs
As loons swim undersea
In and out flickered. Guns
Trained on the woodside, eyes
Covered the Seneschal
Kneeling, ear to the ground,
In whose face, as in the face
Of a physician Hope

And Terror read, they read
His diagnosis. And this,
Rising subdued, he delivered:
'They have struck the trail.'
                    He had heard
What they would hear: a single
Yelp (now they heard it),
Two now, and now twenty,
Now the concerted whine
Scattered at first, and now
Closed up. Not this
The baying which announces
Fox, hare or deer,
But a constant sharp
And broken yelp – the hounds
In sight of the quarry. Yet
The cry ceased, as the pack
Closed with the beast. Unseen
The attack was launched. And the brute
Defended himself, for the cries
Were punctuated often now and often
With the long death howl.

Guns at the ready, bent
Like a bow, each huntsman's head
Pointed. And they could wait
No longer, but they broke
Station, the Seneschal
Shouting unheeded, and moved
Crowding, as from horseback
He promised them all,
Gentle and simple, the lash.
No help for it – they'd see
And all see first. Came three
Shots, then a volley, then
Above the volley, shocking
The woodland echoes, a dreadful
Sound where pain, despair
And fury mixed, the bear's
Tormented roar. And ragged
Behind it yelps,

Cries, and the horns of beaters
All on the move, and all
Except the Seneschal
Exultant.
                    On the one side
They massed; but the beast turned back
To the open fields and the few
Who stayed, the Seneschal,
Tadéusz, the Count, with beaters
Where the wood thinned. A roaring
Within and the crackle of boughs
Came near and nearer.
                              Out
Burst like a thunderbolt
From cloud, the bear!
Torn, with terror
And the dogs upon him,
He stopped, turned, reared
Erect, and with a roar
Quelled his assailants; stooped
His forepaws scrabbling, tore
Roots from the earth and flung them
At dogs and men; uprooted
A tree he flailed like a club,
So turned and came on, rushing
Tadéusz and the Count,
Last of the line. Their muskets,
As lightning rods discharge
At a lowering cloud, discharged
And missed. Four hands together
Seize (the beast still bearing
Down on them) a pike
Planted between them,
Each way tugged at once.

So near to the bear
His double row of tusks
Gleamed on them from his red
Maw, and his claw descended
Upon them, thereupon turning
Through the sparse trees they doubled.

To claw the skull from their brains
As a hat uncovers a head,
The black paw reared. The Assessor
Appeared, and the Notary; Gerwazy
Showed up in front, and Robak
Behind him, running. As
At a command, together
Three shots rang out. Like a hare
Who, the hounds upon him, takes
To the air before them,
So leapt the bear,
Came down head foremost, hurled,
His four paws somersaulting,
His bloody bulk under the Count
And still would rise. The mastiffs
Each side closed upon him.

And now the Seneschal
Had seized his famous horn
That, mottled and involved,
Seemed a great snake. He bore it
To his lips, two-handed. His cheeks
Distended, and as his eyes
Were shot with blood, the lids
Half-veiled them. So he drew
From his pinched-in belly, breath,
And so expelled it. Cyclones
Of whirling air up-spiralled
To roll down and amaze the woods
With purity and volume. For he played
The original catch, the art
For which he was renowned
Of old through the forests: first
The morning call over the kennels,
Then yelps as the kennels were loosed,
The baying pack, and last
The volley sounded.

Here he broke off, but still
He held the horn;
It was the echo playing,
That seemed the Seneschal.

Again he sounded. You thought
The horn at his lips endured
Metamorphoses, swelling
And dwindling as it feigned
Now the bellow of bison
Cutting the wind; now, thickened,
The bear's throat roaring. It thinned
And a wolf's long howling
Came down wind.

Here he broke off, but still
He held the horn:
It was the echo playing,
That seemed the Seneschal.
Oaks to the oaks repeated it,
The beeches to the beeches.

Again he blew. The horn,
It was a hundred horns.
The wrath and terror
Of the men, the pack
And the quarry mingled. Last
The lifted horn pealed
Triumph skyward.

Here he broke off, but still
He held the horn:
It was the echo playing,
That seemed the Seneschal.
And all about the forest,
To every tree a horn.
Trees to the trees, as choirs
Take up from choirs, repeated
The note that broader, further
And fainter spread,
And in the extreme distance
At the sill of heaven expired.

But now his arms were thrown
Wide, and the horn
Fell, swung on a thong;

93

As, cruciform
And swollen-faced, his eyes
Lifted, still he tried
To catch the last and long
Long-drawn
Note from the skies,

As plaudits came to drown
The horn.

'Seneschal leaving the Wood'

Seneschal leaving the wood
Your hunt is over, but hers
In the empty house you return to,
Hers is beginning.
Telimena sits without moving
Folding her arms; but her thoughts
Pursue from a view to a kill
At once, two quarries;
The Count, and Tadeusz.
(And so she gets up from the sofa.
Does she only seem to grow taller,
Parting her bodice, consulting
Sidelong the glass on the wall?)

'However their thoughts may wander
Young men are more constant at heart,
For conscience's sake, than their elders;
She who was first to impart
The sweets of love can expect
From their simple and maidenly feeling,
Long after, a grateful respect.
Youth welcomes and rises from love
As from a modestly planned
Meal that we eat with a friend,
Gaily. Consumed from within,
Only the old debauchee
Detests what he drowns himself in.'

Thus a woman of experience
Reflects on these matters,
Sensibly.
        But white,
In a long white gown,
Turning about as a fountain
Turns among flowers,
Zosia is feeding the fowl.
Over the wings and the heads
Pearl of a white hand, pearl
Of the hail of the barley
Scatters out, dense from the sieve.
Telimena, her guardian,
Summons. She deals them the rest,
Strikes on the sieve as a dancer
Will strike on a tabor, whirling
Striking a strict time. Swooping
Now she flies through the fowl
That scatter before her. Doves,
Doves go before her
As before Venus's car
As she goes, skimming.

Alas how unwise
To augment the advantage of girlhood
With a pitcher of water
Tipped into a basin of silver;
How much too indulgent
Unstoppering flasks from the Nevsky,
Pomade for corn-coloured hair
And scent too sweet for a rival;
Alas, and how rash
White open-work stockings from Warsaw
And white satin shoes,
And braids, the hair smooth on the temples.

In vain to importune a lover
Whose cheeks have paled for a youthful
Small head, once seen, now remembered;
In vain to attempt a diversion
And sharpen a jest on him standing,

Arm on a mantel,
Silent, apart, in a corner;
In vain, when all fail, to upbraid
Till he plunge, like a pike, for his freedom,
Dragging the iron and line.

The Year 1812

Year well remembered! Happy who beheld thee!
The commons knew thee as the year of yield,
But as the year of war, the soldiery.

Rumours and skyward prodigies revealed
The poet's dream, the tale on old men's lips,
The spring when kine preferred the barren field.

Short of the acres green with growing tips
They halted lowing, chewed the winter's cud;
The men awaited an apocalypse.

Languid the farmer sought his livelihood
And checked his team and gazed, as if enquiring
What marvels gathered westward while he stood.

He asked the stork, whose white returning wing
Already spread above its native pine
Had raised the early standard of the Spring.

From swallows gathering frozen mud to line
Their tiny homes, or in loud regiments
Ranged over water, he implored a sign.

The thickets hear each night as dusk descends
The woodcock's call. The forests hear the geese
Honk, and go down. The crane's voice never ends.

What storms have whirled them from what shaken seas,
The watchers ask, that they should come so soon?
Or in the feathered world, what mutinies?

For now fresh migrants of a brighter plume
Than finch or plover gleam above the hills,
Impend, descend, and on our meadows loom.

Cavalry! Troop after troop it spills
With strange insignia, strangely armed,
As snow in a spring thaw fills

The valley roads. From the forests long
Bright bayonets issue, as brigades of foot
Debouch like ants, form up, and densely throng;

All heading north as if the bird, the scout,
Had led men here from halcyon lands, impelled
By instincts too imperative to doubt.

War! the war! – a meaning that transpires
To the remotest corner. In the wood
Beyond whose bounds no rustic mind enquires,

Where in the sky the peasant understood
Only the wind's cry, and on earth the brute's
(And all his visitors the neighbourhood),

A sudden glare! A crash! A ball that shoots
Far from the field, makes its impeded way,
Rips through the branches and lays bare the roots.

The bearded bison trembles, and at bay
Heaves to his forelegs, ruffs his mane, and glares
At sudden sparks that glitter on the spray.

The stray bomb spins and hisses; as he stares,
Bursts. And the beast that never knew alarm
Blunders in panic to profounder lairs.

'Whither the battle?' – and the young men arm.
The women pray, 'God is Napoleon's shield,
Napoleon ours', as to the outcome calm.

Spring well remembered! Happy who saw thee then,
Spring of the war, Spring of the mighty yield,
That promised corn but ripened into men.

★   ★   ★

Out of the moist dark
Dawn without glow brings
Day without brightness.

Sunrise, a whiteness
In a thatch of mist,
Shows late to eastward.

Earth is as tardy;
Cows go to pasture,
Startle hares grazing.

Fog that had spared them
Dayspring's alarum
Dispels them with herds.

Groves where the damp birds
Brood are their havens
In the still woodland.

Storks clack from marshland;
Ravens on haycocks
Croak of wet weather.

Scythes ring together,
Clink of the sickle,
Hone, hammer, and dirge.

Fog at the field's verge
Strangles the echo
Of labour and song.

The bravery of its gentry,
The beauty of their women
Exalt Dobrzyn
Through Lithuania. Once
Six hundred gentry armed
Answered the summons,
The besom made of twigs;
But now no easy living
For gentry of Dobrzyn

In magnates' households,
In troops or at assemblies –
Like serfs they work their way,
Not clad like serfs, the men
In gowns black-striped on white,
In gloves their women spinning
Or leather-shod tending the herds.

All Bartlemies, Matthiases,
Of Polish stock,
Masovian still
In speech and usages,
Black-haired and aquiline,
Nicknamed to save confusion;
Their patriarch, Matthias,
'The Maciek of Macieks';
His house, although untended,
Their Capitol.

Mercury's vivid fringe,
Mullein and crocus bow
The thatch; and mosses tinge
The roof as green as tin.
The rabbit mines below
Windows where birds fly in.
Birdcage or warren now
The fortress of Dobrzyn.

Where once the gate would creak,
Swedes left a cannon ball.
Unhallowed crosses speak
Of sudden obsequies.
Specks swarm on every wall
And seem a rash of fleas;
In each there nests a ball
As in earth burrows, bees.

Innocent every door
Of nail or hook or latch.
(The steel old swordsmen wore
Bit iron, and stood the test

Nor ever showed a notch.)
Above, Dobrzynski crests;
Cheeses the bearings smutch
And swallows blur with nests.

Four helms, once ornaments
Of martial brows, the dove,
Love's votary, frequents;
A corselet of chain mail
Hangs as a chute above
A horse's stall; a tail
Lopped from the charger of
The Ottoman cleans a pail.

Ceres has banished Mars;
Vertumnus and Pomona
And Flora heal the scars
On stable, house and barn.
Today shall they throw over
That distaff rule, and learn
Old habits to recover
To greet the god's return.

★ ★ ★

Fair weather, and the day breaking
Day of our Lady of Flowers;
The sky clear, hung over land
Like a sea curved forward and backward;
Pearls under its wave
Some few stars still, though paling;
White cloudlet alone
(Wing feathers fray out in the azure),
Spirit departing
Belated by prayers,
Fares fast to its heavenly fellows.

Pearls dim and go out in the deep.
Pallor on the sky's brow midmost
Spreads, and one temple is swarthy
Crumpled, pillowed on shadows,

The other ruddy. The distant
Horizon parts like a lid
On the white of an eye
Iris and pupil, and a ray circles
Dazzles, a gold shaft
Stuck through the heart of a cloud.

Fires cluster and dart
Cross over, light over light
Overarches the sky-round;
Drowsy, a broken
Light under lashes shaken
The eye of the sun rose up
Glittered, seven-tinted:
Sapphire by blood is to ruby
Ruby by yellow to topaz
Crystal, by lucent
To diamond, and by flame
Great moon or fitful star.
And the eye of the sun rose up
Alone across the unmeasured.

'Thronged Chapel spills into a Meadow'

Thronged chapel spills into a meadow.
Lowered in worship the heads;
Field of ripe grain
The Lithuanian flaxen;
Girl's head with flowers adorned
Or as ribbons flow loose from a braid,
Cornflower in corn or a poppy;
And the heads sway down
As at a breath of the wind
Over the wheat ears
So to the bell on the wind.

Village girls brought to the altar
Spring's earliest tribute of green,
Sheaves over altar and ikon

Belfry and galleries decked.
Zephyr of morning
Stirring out of the East
Throws down a garland,
Fragrance as of a censer.

Epilogue

How many memories, what long sorrow
There where a man shall cleave to his master
As here no wife cleaves to her man;
There where a man grieves for loss of his weapons
Longer than here for who sired him;
And his tears fall more sincerely and faster
There for a hound than this people's for heroes.

My friends of those days made my speech come easy,
Each good for some singable idiom. Spring
Brought in the fable cranes of the wild island flying
Over the spellbound castle and the spellbound
Boy lamenting, who was loosed
By each pitying bird as it flew, one feather:
He flew out on those wings to his own people.

from *New and Selected Poems* (1961)

Against Confidences

Loose lips now
Call Candour friend
Whom Candour's brow,
When clear, contemned.

Candour can live
Within no shade
That our compulsive
Needs have made

On couches where
We sleep, confess,
Couple and share
A pleased distress.

Not to dispense
With privacies,
But reticence
His practice is;

Agreeing where
Is no denial,
Not to spare
One truth from trial,

But to respect
Conviction's plight
In Intellect's
Hard equal light.

Not to permit,
To shy belief
Too bleakly lit,
The shade's relief

Clouds Candour's brow,
But to indulge
These mouths that now
Divulge, divulge.

Nineteen-Seventeen

A glass in a Liverpool drawing room cracked across.
A telegram fell out of it for Rica.
Perfidious glass that would not mirror loss,
The omen had outstripped the telegram.

A glass in Roscoe's drawing room fell apart
And handed out a telegram from France.
Rica got up from winding bandages.

The gaze of the glass was frantic and averted.
A wet and severed wrist, a hand that shook
Came from the mirror and delivered death
To Liverpool and England in a look.

She reckoned there could not be long to wait.
A wedge of wrack was hunting in from sea
As stadiums spill spectators from a gate.
The thrumming bolt approached her from the blue.
Its piercing note already shattered glass.

A world of plush and leather came to pieces,
Mahogany was shivered into glass.
She smiled farewell to all their startled faces
And steadily outstripped the telegram.

To a Brother in the Mystery

Circa 1290

The world of God has turned its two stone faces
One my way, one yours. Yet we change places
A little, slowly. After we had halved
The work between us, those grotesques I carved
There in the first bays clockwise from the door,
That was such work as I got credit for
At York and Beverley: thorn-leaves twined and bent
To frame some small and human incident

Domestic or of venery. Each time I crossed
Since then, however, underneath the vast
Span of our Mansfield limestone, to appraise
How you cut stone, my emulous hard gaze
Has got to know you as I know the stone
Where none but chisels talk for us. I have grown
Of my own way of thinking yet of yours,
Seeing your leafage burgeon there by the doors
With a light that, flickering, trenches the voussoir's line;
Learning your pre-harmonies, design
Nourished by exuberance, and fine-drawn
Severity that is tenderness, I have thought,
Looking at these last stalls that I have wrought
This side of the chapter's octagon, I find
No hand but mine at work, yet mine refined
By yours, and all the difference: my motif
Of foliate form, your godliness in leaf.
    And your last spandrel proves the debt incurred
Not all on the one side. There I see a bird
Pecks at your grapes, and after him a fowler,
A boy with a bow. Elsewhere, your leaves discover
Of late blank mask-like faces. We infect
Each other then, doubtless to good effect . . .
And yet, take care: this cordial knack bereaves
The mind of all its sympathy with leaves,
Even with stone. I would not take away
From your peculiar mastery, if I say
A sort of coldness is the core of it,
A sort of cruelty; that prerequisite
Perhaps I rob you of, and in exchange give
What? Vulgarity's prerogative,
Indulgence towards the frailties it indulges,
Humour called 'wryness' that acknowledges
Its own complicity. I can keep in mind
So much at all events, can always find
Fallen humanity enough, in stone,
Yes, in the medium; where we cannot own
Crispness, compactness, elegance, but the feature
Seals it and signs it work of human nature
And fallen though redeemable. You, I fear,
Will find you bought humanity too dear

At the price of some light leaves, if you begin
To find your handling of them growing thin,
Insensitive, brittle. For the common touch,
Though it warms, coarsens. Never care so much
For leaves or people, but you care for stone
A little more. The medium is its own
Thing, and not all a medium, but the stuff
Of mountains; cruel, obdurate, and rough.

Killala*

Forlorn indeed Hope on these shores,
White-breeched, under a tricorne, shouting orders
Into the wind in a European language
La gloire against the Atlantic.
                              And Enniscrone,
The unfocussed village carefully grouped on absence . . .

Laden with Europe, toiling up out of the sea
With all the baggage of their own and Europe's
History barnacled, clammy with tawny jellies
And spotted silts, the wreck
Of unwashed hope is a more combustible flotsam
Than this more stranded,
More featureless than any conurbation.

Not memory (her lading) nor the vessel
– No, nor the vessel, for the *Téméraire*
Has been a dozen ships and all one venture –
But the venture persists. Such a temerity,
So bare a chance deserves a barer rock's
Less cluttered landfall. Nakedness
Is structural, asks a binnacle at sea;
By land, if not an oak, a standing stone
Hewn or unhewn in an open place, for the venture
To take a shape by. But the prudent Gael,
Disguised on the skyline as habitation tatters
A scarecrow coast, has blurred identity
By blurring shape, a flutter of rags in the wind.

  * *Killala:* where the French landed in Ireland in 1798.

108

Frenchman, the beacons flare across the Midlands.
Stopping the car and hating this ugly place,
Let this be as if I had lit the first of the beacons,
Of driftwood fetched from the shore,
Announcing your identity and presence:
Not an idea, abstract notion, quality
But a being only, able for life and action,
The same it was some time ago, in France.

With the Grain

I

Why, by an ingrained habit, elevate
        Into their own ideas
Activities like carpentry, become
        The metaphors of graining?
Gardening, the one word, tilth? Or thought,
        The idea of having ideas,
Resolved into images of tilth and graining?

An ingrained habit . . . This is fanciful:
        And there's the rub
Bristling, where the irritable block
        Screams underneath the blade
Of love's demand, or in crimped and gouged-out
        Shavings only, looses
Under a peeling logic its perceptions.

Language (mine, when wounding,
        Yours, back-biting) lacks
No whorl nor one-way shelving. It resists,
        Screams its remonstrance, planes
Reluctantly to a level. And the most
        Reasonable of settlements betrays
Unsmoothed resentment under the caress.

II

The purest hue, let only the light be sufficient
        Turns colour. And I was told

If painters frequent St Ives
    It is because the light
There, under the cliff, is merciful. I dream
    Of an equable light upon words
And as painters paint in St Ives, the poets speaking.

Under that cliff we should say, my dear,
    Not what we mean, but what
The words would mean. We should speak,
    As carpenters work,
With the grain of our words. We should utter
    Unceasingly the hue of love
Safe from the battery of changeable light.

(Love, a condition of such fixed colour,
    Cornwall indeed, or Wales
Might foster. Lovers in mauve,
    Like white-robed Druids
Or the Bards in blue, would need
    A magical philtre, no less,
Like Iseult's, to change partners.)

III

Such a fourth estate of the realm,
    Hieratic unwinking
Mauve or blue under skies steel-silver,
    Would chamfer away
A knot in the grain of a streaming light, the glitter,
    Off lances' points, that moved
A sluggish Froissart to aesthetic feeling.

And will the poet, carpenter of light,
    Work with the grain henceforward?
If glitterings won't fetch him
    Nor the refractory crystal,
Will he never again look into the source of light
    Aquiline, but fly
Always out of the sun, unseen till softly alighting?

Why, by an ingrained habit, elevate
    Into the light of ideas

The colourful trades, if not like Icarus
    To climb the beam? High lights
Are always white, but this ideal sun
    Dyes only more intensely, and we find
Enough cross-graining in the most abstract nature.

Red Rock of Utah

of golde and sylver they make commonly chaumber pottes, and
other vesselles, that serve for moste vile uses. . . .
Furthermore of the same mettalles they make greate chaines,
fetters, and gieves wherin they tie their bondmen.
Finally whosoever for anye offense be inflamed, by their eares hang
rynges of golde, upon their fyngers they weare rynges of golde,
and aboute their neckes chaines of golde, and in conclusion their
heades be tied aboute with gold.   More's Utopia

Surely it has some virtue, having none,
Sighed to her bondman the Utopian lady
Telling the links of gold among his hair.
At wrist and ankle, fingers, head and neck
The unserviceable metal he must wear
In rings, chains, chainmail bonnets, riveted
Locked, knotted, wound on him whom her affection
Chose she conceived perversely; till she guessed
Its virtue was in helmeting that head,
A collar round the neck she hung upon.

      What colour were Utopia's rocks?
      Navajo red, the Mormon wives
      Mutter, restless in drab smocks,
      Would void the golden chamberpots
      And strike off the golden gyves
      In crimson Zion. Under the mesa's
      Coronet, taken from such base uses,
      Shall not red gold deck the wives of Utah?

      'Convicting us, convict the Lord
      Of barbarous inutilities:
      What left His hand but a very gaud,

Red over canyon and mesa, good
For nothing but an artifice
To adorn His favoured? Little we ask
Who wintered for Him in Nebraska:
Red gold only, a little at wrist or ankle.'

'Has it then every virtue, having none?'
Sighs to the Lord in prayer the Mormon lady
And Nephi Johnson remonstrates, 'What good
The land, if not for cotton?' But the Lord,
Dear reverend pioneers, in His red blood
Sealed more than that hard promise of a sod
To turn in Zion. Planting such dubious
Capacities in your sons as might applaud
Gauds of gratuitous ornament in your God,
Your God depraved King Utopus himself.

Reflections on Deafness

For Kenneth and Margaret Millar

I

Making the best and most of a visitation,
The deaf can make it serve their purposes.
What else can any one use but his condition?
Is affliction turned to use the less affliction?

II

The voice called ours, played back to us on tape,
We hate at once, disown. The nerve of selfhood
Jumps at the drill of an achieved imposture.
The deaf cannot tell the King from the Pretender.

III

The blind have rights in that most delicate
And intimate of the senses, touch; the deaf
Lip-reader, in somnambulistic rape
On the act of sight, usurps the rights denied him.

Blindness that can be rectified by reason,
Errors of calculation not in will
We tolerate; but wince to see the human,
Distinguishingly human act of speech contorted.

IV

Yes, we are deaf to their condition, hear
All that we want to hear, the blind man's stick
Redeemably tap-tapping, but the voice
That cannot hear itself we cannot hear.

For an Age of Plastics

With the effect almost of carving the hillside
     They climb in their stiff terraces, these houses
Feed the returning eye with national pride
     In the 'built to last.' Approving elegance
Where there is only decency, the eye
     Applauds the air of nothing left to chance
Or brilliantly provisional. Not the fact
     But the air of it, the illusion, we observe;
Chance in the bomb sight kept these streets intact
     And razed whole districts. Nor was the lesson lost
On the rebuilt Plymouth, how an age of chance
     Is an age of plastics. In a style pre-cast
Pre-fabricated, and as if its site
     Were the canyon's lip, it rises out of rubble
Sketchily massive, moulded in bakelite.

Annoyed to take a gloomy sort of pride
     In numbering our losses, I suppose
The ploughman ceased his carving of the hillside
     And all the coulters and the chisels broke
When he was young whom we come home to bury,
     A man like clay in the hands of his womenfolk.

A ploughman carved three harvests, each a son,
     Upon the flesh of Wales. And all were carried
Long since from those hillsides, yet this one

Comes first to threshing. Nutriment and grain
For all the mashing of the interim
　　　Live in the load of him. Living again
His shipwright's years, the countryman's walks in the park,
　　　The scrape of a mattock in a too small garden,
The marriage to the capable matriarch,
　　　What would he change? Perhaps a stubbornness
That bristled sometimes, for the sensible hands
　　　To circumvent and gentle, would be less
Amenable to their shaping. But all told,
　　　His edged tools still would lie in the garden shed,
Still he would flow, himself, from mould to mould.

Whatever he showed of something in the rough,
　　　Sluggish in flow and unadaptable,
I liked him for; affecting to be gruff,
　　　An awkward customer – so much was due,
He seemed to think, to what a man was, once:
　　　Something to build with, take a chisel to.

The Life of Service

Service, or Latin *sorbus*, European
More especially English shadbush or small tree,
Asks all the shade the fancier can find
In a walled garden. This is no plebeian
Of cottage plots, though coarse in leaf and rind.

Planted, it is persistent, of a thick
Skin, and grows strong the more it's trodden on;
Or afterwards, as an established upas,
Thrives all the better by each welcomed nick
Of aggrieved knives wielded by interlopers.

By this indeed it knows itself. Self-thwarted,
It welcomes parasites, for playing host
To what insults and saps it is its virtue
And its fulfilment. Flourishing contorted,
All its long-suffering's overbearing too.

Some cultivators hold that it repays,
By its small edible fruit (in favoured species
Of a vinous taste), its culture. It does not;
All saner growth abhors it, and the Bays
Wither, affronted, in the poisoned plot.

The 'Sculpture' of Rhyme

Potter nor iron-founder
Nor caster of bronze will he cherish,
But the monumental mason;

As if his higher stake
Than the impregnable spiders
Of self-defended music

Procured him mandibles
To chisel honey from the saxifrage,
And a mouth to graze on feldspar.

A Sequence for Francis Parkman (1961)

The Jesuits in North America

Récollet friars and the very Huguenots were as often as Jesuits Champlain's companions on early investigations of the seaboard of Acadia and the estuary of the St Lawrence river. It was not at his instigation, though it was with his compliance, that the Canadian mission, big with a harvest of monstrous and astonishing martyrdoms, became a monopoly of the Society of Jesus.

Curé and pastor, dead at the one time
Buried in the one grave
To see would they lie peaceable together
Who never lived so on Acadia's coast;
And the Aeneas of a destined nation
Sees uses for recalcitrance,
No matter priest or pastor,
Sectarian zeal to rib the rock, Quebec.

Only the holy fathers were
Holy and resolute enough
To live in Huron lodges;
Only the wily fathers could
Only the holy fathers
Outwit the Iroquois.

Saguenay, Ohio, Colorado
Roll gloomy waters, and the Ottawa
Plunging, boiled. Shot spray from that concussion
Smoked out of Champlain's arquebuse
In Indian wars; he knew
A demon in the cataract. Tobacco
Disbursed on foam placates the Manitou.

Only the holy fathers were
Holy and resolute enough;
Devils and devildom
Incarnate, none but they,
The incarnate God's
Adepts and ministers,
Might recognize and slay.

Savages convert the savages.

Canoe that darted out upon the still
Bay of the Trinity, dark as Acheron,
Sanctuary of solitude and silence,
The soul of Champlain, dying, took such forms
As never a Jesuit of France could tell;
More shapes than one, since all were Canada.

At Sainte-Marie the fathers' mail from France
Accumulates unread. The holy fathers
Only the holy fathers
Were resolute for martyrdom. Apache,
Last suicidal chieftain in a column
Of blowing dust, a dry soil's levity
Too late affects the Roman.
Fatuity not cowardice undid
The Huron nation, and intractable
Indolence the Iroquois. But all
Had seen too many gods, as I have seen them
Too many, and too different. There is
No God but One and He is terrible
Dwells in the Huron lodges
Outwits the Iroquois.

Lasalle

Lasalle who, for no sordid end, pressing to the waters of the
Mississippi, first by that watery highway attained to the
Gulf of Mexico, was a spirit cold and stern.
His followers, who shared his perplexities and endured the
effects of his perseverance, at most respected, always feared, and
never loved him; a truth sufficiently attested by the
circumstances of his obscure death at their mutinous hands
in the deserts of Louisiana. In his letters written to his creditors and
friends, he has confessed that the wilderness drew him not otherwise
than as a theatre for his restless ambitions, where they
would be less obstructed than in the palaces and faubourgs of
Paris by a lack of that conversibility and address which
alone, in a more civil society, can recommend and please.

Of this aspiring burgher who disdained
(Dumb in his pride of mortified reserve)
The usufruct of half a continent,

After the dark inexorable river
Delivers him the salt breath of the sea,
Still we complain: Dark it was not, until
He made it so, inexorable, nor fatal.

He loved solitude and he loved power
And Parkman loves him for it. Better love
Profit: if no principle nor faith
Move his lids' mountains, cannot Trade unsheet
The gathered waters of five inland oceans,
A prodigal Nature's parks and pleasure grounds,
Wild swans, wild turkeys, cranes and pelicans?

He never saw it, any of it: saw
The Mississippi that was bright, as dark,
Indifferent, as inexorable; saw
(As if in those accounts he never kept)
Digits and proxies, lean alternatives
To audiences with a Monseigneur
Where he had lacked complaisance and address.

He loved solitude and he loved power
And lonely as when born of chaos, bright
Voiceless, sail-less, without sign of life
The great Gulf opened, tossing – but what for?
Not for the Faith, for glory, or for France,
Whirled on the miry vortex of his need,
The light canoes of Indian nations foundered.

Frontenac

*In what was wilderness as inviolate then as in the last
century were the gorges of the High Sierra when revealed to
the astonished gaze of the intrepid John Muir,
the Marquis of Frontenac founded three hundred years ago the
rude fortress of which the all but obliterated site still, though
uncertainly, preserves his name in the city of Kingston, Ontario.
There, however, a hundred will ask for Old Fort Henry,
the surviving British edifice, for the one curious traveller who
enquires after the remains of Fort Frontenac.*

The adjacent terrain is that which the pen of Fenimore Cooper
has made interesting to all amateurs of the sublime and
romantic by the adventures of the immortal Chingachgook,
in romances which, if written in a manner no less orotund,
reveal also a genius as copious and spirited as the productions
of the author of 'Waverley'. Yet however stirring and
authentic the narrative, it must inevitably fail in delineating
scenes of which the impressive charm is precisely that they
were for so long untrodden, unless rarely by the moccasin of the
savage and solitary hunter, and celebrated only by the wind's
pencil and the music of the cataract.
It was not by the force of arms, but by the framing of
fraudulent contracts and the sale of spirituous liquours,
that these territories were wrested from their original dusky
citizens.

Hearing from some how the Sierra answers
Even today, to John Muir's nails and rifle,
With human resonances,
I heard the long-tamed wilderness give back
Over the Lake and all too British Kingston
The one word, 'Frontenac.'
But after-echoes mocked: The rocky flanges
Of the Thousand Islands
Have more to do than take up challenges
From perfect strangers;
Agoraphobia among empty spaces,
The mountain ranges, the plains of corn,
Peoples the street at history's intersections
With famous faces.

Heart of Midlothian, the milky mother
(Sir Walter's Doric) of sane masterpieces
Fed at that flaccid udder, Walter Scott,
Great lax geometer, first plotted them,
Triangulations that explode
The architect's box of space, and by a torsion
As bland as violent sprain
Narrative time and the archives' single slot.

What's to be seen of old Fort Frontenac?
The British fortress, by a hundred years
More recent, but still Old
Fort Henry, draws the Buicks. Of the Frenchman

A mound remains by Kingston's waterfront
And a cadence out of Parkman: 'At Versailles
A portrait, beautiful and young, Minerva . . .'

Intervals in what never meets the eye
Meet the ear sooner, music's images
Not of Ontario's spaces but of spaces
Sketched by a gesture, virtual and French.

Alas for Caliban. The Thousand Islands
Were full of noises,
Landscape and history echoing back and forth
Under immense skies, till his master
Cabined his spaces in a folio
And Euclids of the tepee, leaning-to
Birch-pole isosceles in a glade of hemlocks,
Drank deafening whisky in a written treaty.

Montcalm

*It is reported of General Wolfe that as he drifted by night to the
secret assault of the Heights of Abraham he quoted to his
companions some famous stanzas of the elegy of Gray.
The French and the British commander were alike destined to die
on the morrow, and thus to illustrate the melancholy truth of the
poet's reflections. Montcalm was himself a poet, and appended
pious verses in French and Latin to a cross erected on his field of
victory at Ticonderoga. He had the sentiments and inclinations of a
country gentleman.
He died before he could learn which of his children had pre-deceased him.*

In Candiac by Nîmes in Languedoc
He left a mill to grind his olives well
Who now must harvest laurels. Who had died
In Candiac? All Bougainville could tell
Was of a death. Mirète he thought had died
If it was Mirète. He never could decide
For whom the olives sighed in Languedoc.

To Candiac by Nîmes in Languedoc
A murmur reaches from the perjured wave
That floats surprise and France's great reverse:

At dawn, too late, the cliffs will answer back.
'The paths of glory lead but to the grave'
– Marmoreal verses, plumes to tuft a hearse
And scutcheons black for squires of Candiac.

From Candiac by Nîmes in Languedoc
Quoting Corneille – 'though, Christian! not Montcalm
Nor his sagacity nor up-ended trees
Nor men nor deeds checked England, but God's arm' –
Coming from this and homelier pieties
In Candiac by Nîmes in Languedoc
To earn the stucco tribute of a plaque,

Montcalm had met, if we should say his match,
We ought to mean his match in hardihood
Hardly in grace, James Wolfe, but most of all
His match in fate, his double. Did he catch
If not the low voice, still its tone, the mood?
The paths of glory led to Quebec
From Candiac by Nîmes in Languedoc.

Both earned their stucco. Marble was reserved
To honour the intrepid, the serene
And the successful Amherst. But it served,
Pompous and frigid as it was, the phrase
'A martial glory': common ground between
The public lives, the private, Kent, Quebec,
And Candiac by Nîmes in Languedoc.

Pontiac

Of all the savages of North America,
history records none more eminent for great
abilities than Pontiac, a sachem of the Ottawas.
He refused to acknowledge the capitulation of
Canada. Inflamed by him, a league of all the
Western tribes invested the ceded forts,
burned many, and massacred the garrisons.
At Detroit, the most considerable of these places,
he was repulsed. But not without justice does

the modern metropolis recall, by the names she
accords the products of her manufactories,
not only her founder, Lamothe-Cadillac, but
also him who would, in the name of his violated
nation, have razed her to the ground.

Pontiac fires Detroit!
On Fort Duquesne afresh
The immaculate lilies! Turn,
Minavavana or
Le Grand Sauteur, and see
Behind the trader's knife
Plunging, *coureurs de bois*
Roll through the fired stockade
The unmentionable chapter –
Extermination of the Seminole,
Deportation of the Cherokee,
Transportation of the Saginaw . . .
A modern miracle of
Engineering fires
Detroit and Cadillac
Where, cast in steel
Or punched out of chrome
On a spinning wheel,
Freely may roam
This totem, this
Served, furbished car
With a name that's his,
Ranging so far:
Pontiac, Ottawa shade.

Bougainville

Lewis de Bougainville, lieutenant to the Marquis of Montcalm
at the fall of Canada, later essayed to annex the Falkland Islands.
*   Baulked of this object by the more politic arrangements of His*
Most Christian Majesty, his next and most extraordinary
venture for the glory of the French nation was a circumnavigation
of the globe in the years 1766, 1767, 1768 and 1769.
*   See his narrative of this voyage, made into English by*
Mr Forster; and the later extension of this work
by the celebrated Diderot, a supplement more ingenious than useful.

All the soft runs of it, the tin-white gashes
Over the muscled mesh and interaction
Of the South Seas tilt against him less unsteady
Than France had been, or a King who could destroy
Acadia sold, Montcalm betrayed by faction,
And all the meadows of the Illinois
Lost, the allies abandoned. Where the ashes
Still smoulder on the ceded Falklands, these
Islands and oceans he has failed already
Though he will navigate the seven seas.

The shame persists as scruple. The exact
Conscience of science chastens observations,
And the redaction of a log-book's soundings
Is scrupulously dry. Although the scent
Carries from Otaheite, can a nation's
Chagrin or honour weigh in the intent
Scrutiny of the sextant? Matter of fact
Dries the great deeps. And yet what tumults when
He marks the fathoms, what disorders, houndings
Of mortification, angers, drive the pen!

No accuracy there but testifies
To a concern behind it, to a feeling
In excess of its object, fact. Excesses
Of that concern (where God permits the pox
And a King is perjured) self-inflict their steeling
To this impassive dryness charting rocks,
Keys, and the set of tide-rips. Weather eyes
Whittled so blue by pains, exactitude
In the science, navigation, witnesses
To the heart's intentions answered, not eschewed.

Needing to know is always how to learn;
Needing to see brings sightings; steadiest readings
Are those that wishes father. In their ages
Of Eden's gold the archipelagos
Await his keel because he wants for Edens
Who held savannahs once and the Ohio's
Bison for France. The measure of concern

Measures the truth, and in the *philosophe*
A paradox of noble savages
Has met no need more urgent than to scoff.

A Letter to Curtis Bradford

Curtis, you've been American too long,
You don't know what it feels like. You belong,
Don't you, too entirely to divulge?
Indifferently therefore you indulge
My idle interests: Are there names perhaps
In Iowa still, to match the names on maps,
Burgundian or Picard voyageurs
Prowling the wilderness for France and furs
On the Des Moines river? And suppose there were
What would it prove? To whom would it occur
In Iowa that, suppose it so, New France
Not your New England has pre-eminence
If to belong means anything? Your smile
(Twisted) admits it doesn't. Steadily, while
You on the seaboard, they in Canada
Dribbled from floods of European war
Boiled in small pools, pressure built up behind
The dams of Europe. Dispossessed mankind,
Your destined countrymen, milled at dock-gates;
Emigrant schooners spilled aboard the States;
The dispossessed, the not to be possessed,
The alone and equal, peopled all the West.
And so what is it I am asking for,
Sipping at names? Dahcotah, Ottawa,
Horse Indian . . . Yes, but earlier (What is this
Need that I find to fill void centuries?)
Who first put up America to let?
You of the old stock paid him rent. And yet
Even so soon, crowds of another sort
Piled off the boats to take him by assault.
And a worse sort, the heroes. Who but they,
For whom the manifest was shadow-play
Of an all-absorbing inward war and plight,
Could so deny its presence and its right?

It was the given. But I only guess,
I guess at it out of my Englishness
And envy you out of England. Man with man
Is all our history; American,
You met with spirits. Neither white nor red
The melancholy, disinherited
Spirit of mid-America, but this,
The manifested copiousness, the bounties.

For Doreen. A Voice from the Garden

from *New Lines*, 2 (1963)

We have a lawn of moss.
The next house is called The Beeches.
A towering squirrel-haunted
Trellis of trees, across
Our matt and trefoil, reaches
Shade where our guests have sauntered.

Cars snap by in the road.
In a famous photographed village
The High Street is our address.
Our guests write from abroad
Delighted to envisage
Rose-arbour and wilderness.

They get them, and the lilacs.
Some frenzy in us discards
Lilacs and all. It will harden,
However England stacks
Her dear discoloured cards
Against us, us to her garden.

Anglophobia rises
In Brooklyn to hysteria
At some British verses.
British, one sympathizes.
Diesel-fumes cling to wistaria.
One conceives of worse reverses.

The sough of the power brake
Makes every man an island;
But we are the island race.
We must be mad to take
Offence at our poisoned land
And the gardens that pock her face.

Trumpington

Events and Wisdoms (1964)

Two Dedications

1   Wide France

Sunlight so blurred with clouds we couldn't tell
Light from shade, driving to Vézelay
Disgusted you that Northern day. You thought
Caressing weather started at Calais,

And I had thought, in Burgundy; and still,
When we had stolen guiltily from where
Mummy lay wretched in the loud hotel,
All we found was squall-dashed street and square.

Nothing to do but go to Vézelay
That afternoon. Both worried, and the seasons
Wrong as usual, winter in our bones,
We drove the ten miles for the worst of reasons.

Let me remind you. First there was a strong
High, famous church; and where the hillside falls
Away behind it, France was spread at our feet;
And at our back old streets and gates and walls.

Poor eight-year-old, but how could you remember?
So many, before and since; and such a fuss
As we always made, as if to convince ourselves.
And now you worry about the eleven-plus.

2   Barnsley Cricket Club

Now the heat comes, I am demoralized.
Important letters lie unanswered, dry
Shreds of tobacco spike the typewriter,
No undertaking but is ill-advised.

Unanswerable even the shortest missive,
Replies not sealed, or sealed without conviction.
Thumb-marks dry out, leaving the paper pouchy,
Tousled with effort, desperate, inconclusive.

'A thing worth doing is worth doing well,'
Says Shaw Lane Cricket Ground
Between the showers of a July evening,
As the catch is held and staid hand-clappings swell.

This almost vertical sun, this blur of heat,
All stinging furze and snagged unravelling,
Denies the axiom which has kept
My father's summers shadowy and sweet.

Remembering many times when he has laughed
Softly, and slapped his thigh, because the trap
So suavely set was consummately sprung,
I wish, to all I love, his love of craft.

Hard to instruct myself, and then my son,
That things which would be natural are done
After a style less consummate; that an art's
More noble office is to leave half-done.

How soon the shadows fall, how soon and long!
The score-board stretches to a grandson's feet.
This layabout July in another climate
Ought not to prove firm turf, well-tended, wrong.

Resolutions

Whenever I talk of my art
You turn away like strangers,
Whereas all I mean is the chart
I keep, of my own sea-changes.

It puzzles the wisest head
How anyone's good resolution
Can securely be implemented;
Art provides a solution.

This is the assessor whose word
Can always be relied on;
It tells you when has occurred
Any change you decide on.

More preciously still, it tells
Of growth not groped towards,
In the seaway a sound of bells
From a landfall not on the cards.

Life Encompassed

How often I have said,
'This will never do,'
Of ways of feeling that now
I trust in, and pursue!

Do traverses tramped in the past,
My own, criss-crossed as I forge
Across from another quarter
Speak of a life encompassed?

Well, life is not research.
No one asks you to map the terrain,
Only to get across it
In new ways, time and again.

How many such, even now,
I dismiss out of hand
As not to my purpose, not
Unknown, just unexamined.

Hornet

In lilac trained on the colonnade's archway, what
Must be a hornet volleys lethally back
And forth in the air, on the still not hot
But blindingly white Italian stone, blue-black.

I have seldom seen them in England, although once
Years ago the foul-mouthed, obligingly bowed
Rat-catcher of Cambridge made a just pretence
To a cup of tea, for a nest cleared in the road.

Those were wasp-coloured, surely; and this blue,
Gun-metal blue, blue-black ominous ranger
Of Italy's air means an Italy stone all through,
Where every herb of holier thought's a stranger.

No call for such rage in our England of pierced shadows.
Stone's and the white sun's opposite, furious fly,
There no sun strides in a rapid creak of cicadas
And the green mould stains before the mortar is dry.

Housekeeping

From thirty years back my grandmother with us boys
Picking the ash-grimed blackberries, pint on pint, is
Housekeeping Yorkshire's thrift, and yet the noise
Is taken up from Somerset in the 'nineties.

From homestead Autumns in the vale of Chard
Translated in youth past any hope of returning,
She toiled, my father a baby, through the hard
Fellside winters, to Barnsley, soused in the Dearne.

How the sound carries! Whatever the dried-out, lank
Sticks of poor trees could say of the slow slag stealing
More berries than we did, I hear her still down the bank
Slide, knickers in evidence, laughing, modestly squealing.

And I hear not only how homestead to small home echoes
Persistence of historic habit. Berries
Ask to be plucked, and attar pleases the rose.
Contentment cries from the distance. How it carries!

Low Lands

I could not live here, though I must and do
Ungratefully inhabit the Cambridgeshire fens
And the low river delta we pass through
Is beautiful in the same uncertain sense.

Like a snake it is, its serpentine iridescence
Of slow light spilt and wheeling over calm
Inundations, and a snake's still menace
Hooding with bruised sky belfry and lonely farm.

The grasses wave on meadows fat with foison.
In granges, cellars, granaries, the rat
Runs sleek and lissom. Tedium, a poison,
Swells in the sac for the hillborn, dwelling in the flat.

How defenceless it is! How much it needs a protector
To keep its dykes! At what a price it commands
The delightful bizarre when it wears like a bus-conductor
Tickets of brown sails tucked into polders' hat-bands!

But a beauty there is, noble, dependent, unshrinking,
In being at somebody's mercy, wide and alone.
I imagine a hillborn sculptor suddenly thinking
One could live well in a country short of stone.

Green River

Green silk, or a shot silk, blue
Verging to green at the edges,
The river reflects the sky
Alas. I wish that its hue
Were the constant green of its sedges
Or the reeds it is floating by.

It reflects the entrances, dangers,
Exploits, vivid reversals
Of weather over the days.

But it learns to make these changes
By too many long rehearsals
Of overcasts and greys.

So let it take its station
Less mutably. Put it to school
Not to the sky but the land.
This endless transformation,
Because it is beautiful,
Let some of it somehow stand.

But seeing the streak of it quiver
There in the distance, my eye
Is astonished and unbelieving.
It exclaims to itself for ever:
This water is passing by!
It arrives, and it is leaving!

House-martin

I see the low black wherry
Under the alders rock,
As the ferryman strides from his ferry
And his child in its black frock

Into his powerful shadow
And out of it, skirmishing, passes
Time and again as they go
Up through the tall lush grasses.

The light of evening grieves
For the stout house of a father,
With martins under its eaves,
That cracks and sags in the weather.

Treviso, the Pescheria

Each of us has the time,
And both the times are wrong.
Our needs and likings chime
Sometimes, but not for long.

Your watch is often fast,
Mine usually slow.
And yet you cling to the past,
I laxly let it go.

You are like a ferryman's daughter,
And I the stream that blurred
Calls sent across that water,
Which loyally you have heard.

My lapsings I acknowledge.
And yet, on either hand
Combed green, the river's sedge
Sweetens the fish-wives' island.

The Prolific Spell

Day by day, such rewards,
Compassionate land!
Such things to say, and the words
And ways of saying to hand!

Bounties I cannot earn!
Nothing planned in advance!
Well, it is hard to learn,
This profiting by chance.

It is hard, learning to live
While looking the other way,
Bored and contemplative
Over a child at play.

Not every one has a child.
All children grow away.
Sufferings drive us wild;
Not every mind can stray.

Nothing engendered, and so much
Constantly brought to birth!
This hand will lose its touch.
Profuse, illiberal earth!

Nothing could be planned
And so no credit accrues.
Ah compassionate land!
Such gain, and nothing to lose!

My utterance that turns
To always human use
Your brilliant mute concerns
Neither repays nor earns.

A Battlefield

Red mills and farms clumped soothingly here and there.
At a modest distance rose a plume of trees
On the green-bushed plain, and had from afar the air
Which poplars have in the pluck of a river breeze:

The crossing of the Piave! In what year
How many times, and by whose army, going
In which direction – none of this was clear;
With a sinking heart I felt it was not worth knowing.

A necropolis and a stand of cypress came
Predictably next, and all of it I knew
Was a peeling village with the curious name,
Victory, and fast traffic passing through.

The Cypress Avenue

My companion kept exclaiming
At fugitive aromas;
She was making a happy fuss
Of flower-naming.

And I, who had taken her there . . .
Not one scent could I name
In the resinous die-straight avenue's
Plume-irrigated air.

Her world was properly indexed:
The names were in my head
Familiar, double-columned, but
Hardly a page of text.

Just the swaying channel of shade;
The stippling everywhere
Of an otherwise dust-choked country;
The difference cypress made.

★   ★   ★

That night at the family sing-song
She had no repertoire;
Her ear was a true one, though
Her voice not very strong.

And that was an index too!
Hymns, shanties, popular numbers,
Ballads, rounds – how many
It turned out that we knew!

And what an encyclopaedia
Of smudged ill-printed feeling
They opened up, although to
Only a coarsened ear.

Humanly Speaking

After two months, already
My auspiciously begun
Adventure of blessing the world
Was turning woe-begone.

Still it might work out, I thought:
The hand-to-mouth way I live,
Not life itself, might be
What made me apprehensive.

But a truce to pieties!
I pull myself together
And get exasperated:
Damn this stupid weather!

So stupid, so uncreative . . .
I am rasped by a towel of wind
And boomed at by grey-green breakers
For seventy-two hours on end.

The weather invades me, throws
My every sense out of gear:
I cannot trust what I see
Or smell or taste or hear.

And because life itself
Is this one soured life I am leading,
And living it hand-to-mouth is
Natural, humanly speaking,

To swear at this barren fig-tree,
At seas uninventively breaking
In self-same pothers, becomes
A duty, humanly speaking.

But I, who had hoped no more
To have to point the finger,
Who had ventured on new feelings . . .
For me misgivings linger.

The Hill Field

Look there! What a wheaten
Half-loaf, halfway to bread,
A cornfield is, that is eaten
Away, and harvested:

How like a loaf, where the knife
Has cut and come again,
Jagged where the farmer's wife
Has served the farmer's men,

That steep field is, where the reaping
Has only just begun
On a wedge-shaped front, and the creeping
Steel edges glint in the sun.

See the cheese-like shape it is taking,
The sliced-off walls of the wheat
And the cheese-mite reapers making
Inroads there, in the heat?

It is Brueghel or Samuel Palmer,
Some painter, coming between
My eye and the truth of a farmer,
So massively sculpts the scene.

The sickles of poets dazzle
These eyes that were filmed from birth;
And the miller comes with an easel
To grind the fruits of earth.

The Feeders

Among the serviceable mills and
The galleries of riverside poplars,
In the holiday house, no hours
Were set aside for my writing;
It was less well-appointed than ours,
But Art found it inviting.

In that impelled present, a weight
Of water behind it, Art
And Life fed into each other:
Children who could not know
How uniquely their mother
Assisted, themselves did so,

On their long serpentine
Of that full river,
Simply by making demands.
Art liked that changeable weather.
I had only one pair of hands;
They held more, cupped together.

Now I must feed myself
On feelings fresh from their source,
Flashfloods tapped in the highlands
Under the glare of noon.
Still only one pair of hands,
And I have to hold the spoon.

In the uplands the stony beds
Chalk-white under vacant bridges . . .
My public has shrunk to one reader,
And that the most exacting,
The hateful, insatiable feeder,
Art; and the rest, play-acting.

A Lily at Noon

Deep-sea frost, and
Lilies at noon . . .
Late leaves, late leaves
Toss every day.
The daymoon shines always for some.
In the marriage of a slow man
Eighteen years is soon.

Sun and moon, no
Dark between,
Foresight and hindsight
Halving the hours.
And now he collects his thoughts
Before it is too late.
But what can 'too late' mean?

Shielding with hands,
Binding to stakes . . .
Late leaves, late leaves
Toss every day,
The sun moves on from noon.
To freeze, to cup, to retard –
These measures terror takes.

Love and the Times

A knowledge of history fetches
Love out of its recesses,
Mapping its open stretches,
Its pits for trespassers.

Or it is staked out there,
For country airs to breathe
On seed-bed and parterre
Savour of field and heath.

Strange how we can imagine
Nothing else, although
We have no hope for the short run
That times can turn out so.

Across the Bay

A queer thing about those waters: there are no
Birds there, or hardly any.
I did not miss them, I do not remember
Missing them, or thinking it uncanny.

The beach so-called was a blinding splinter of limestone,
A quarry outraged by hulls.
We took pleasure in that: the emptiness, the hardness
Of the light, the silence, and the water's stillness.

But this was the setting for one of our murderous scenes.
This hurt, and goes on hurting:
The venomous soft jelly, the undersides.
We could stand the world if it were hard all over.

A Christening

What we do best is breed:
August Bank Holiday, whole
Populations explode

Across the wolds and in a slot
Of small cars pullulate
By couples. Millington Meadows

Flower with campstools. At
Beverley the font
Has a cover carved like a goblet.

The new baby is fed.
I stumble back to bed.
I hear the owls for a long time

Hunting. Or are they never
In the winter grey of before dawn,
Those pure long quavers,

Cries of love? I put my arms around you.
Small mice freeze among tussocks.
The baby wails in the next room.

Upstairs Mrs Ramsden
Dies, and the house
Is full of the cries of the newborn.

In red and smoky wood
A follower of Wren
Carved it at Beverley:

The generous womb that drops
Into the sanctified water immediate fruit.
What we do best is breed.

Agave in the West

I like the sidewalks of an American city,
Broad shadowed stone. I think of Agave,

Queen of the maenads, after incestuous fury
Shocked and quiescent, pleading for the cage:
Grids of a rectilinear plot, her cities.

Leaving the wilderness, she counts the loss
Of a world of signs – in algae, moss,
Guano, lichen, all the blooms of stone;
In cross-grained baulks and boles, in timber grown
Noble in groves or into monstrous shapes;
In rock-formations, cloud-formations, landscapes.
I like the sidewalks of an American city:

Sunstruck solitude of parking lots;
Taut vivid women, hair close-shaved from the armpit;
Glass walls run up, run out on the canyon's lip.
Barber my verses, pitiless vivid city.

In California

Chemicals ripen the citrus;
There are rattlesnakes in the mountains,
And on the shoreline
Hygiene, inhuman caution.

Beef in cellophane
Tall as giraffes,
The orange-rancher's daughters
Crop their own groves, mistrustful.

Perpetual summer seems
Precarious on the littoral. We drive
Inland to prove
The risk we sense. At once

Winter claps-to like a shutter
High over the Ojai valley, and discloses
A double crisis,
Winter and Drought.

Ranges on mountain-ranges,
Empty, unwatered, crumbling,
Hot colours come at the eye.
It is too cold

For picnics at the trestle-tables. Claypit
Yellow burns on the distance.
The phantom walks
Everywhere, of intolerable heat.

At Ventucopa, elevation
Two-eight-nine-six, the water hydrant frozen,
Deserted or broken settlements,
Gasoline stations closed and boarded.

By nightfall, to the snows;
And over the mile on tilted
Mile of the mountain park
The bright cars hazarded.

New York in August

(After Pasternak)

There came, for lack of sleep,
A crosspatch, drained-out look
On the old trees that keep
Scents of Schiedam and the Hook

In Flushing, as we picked out, past
Each memorized landmark,
Our route to a somnolent breakfast.
Later, to Central Park,

UNO, and the Empire State.
A haven from the heat
Was the Planetarium. We got back late,
Buffeted, dragging our feet.

Clammy, electric, torrid,
The nights bring no relief
At the latitude of Madrid.
Never the stir of a leaf

Any night, as we went
Back, the children asleep,
To our bed in a loaned apartment,
Although I thought a deep

And savage cry from the park
Came once, as we flashed together
And the fan whirled in the dark,
For thunder, a break in the weather.

Viper-Man

Will it be one of those
Forever summers?
Will the terrace stone
Expand, unseal
Aromas, and let slip
Out of the cell of its granulations
Some mid-Victorian courtship?

Never a belle of that
Lavender century
But, though so stayed,
Basked in a settled spell;
And yet I guard
Against a change in the weather,
Snake whipped up in the yard.

In Chopin's Garden

I remember the scarlet setts
Of the little-frequented highway
From Warsaw to the West
And Chopin's house, one Sunday.

I remember outside the windows,
As the pianist plucked a ring
From her thin white finger, the rows
Of unanchored faces waiting,

And a climbing vapour, storm-wrack
Wreathing up, heavy with fruit,
Darkened the skies at their back
On the old invasion-route.

Masovia bows its birches
Resignedly. Again
A rapid army marches
Eastward over the plain,

And fast now it approaches.
Turbulence, agonies,
As the poised musician broaches
The polonaise, storm from the keys.

See them, ennobled by
The mass and passage, these
Faces stained with the sky,
Supple and fluid as trees.

Poreč

Pennies of sun's fire jazzing like silver foil,
In this off-shore pleasaunce of Croatia
Leased to the Sports Club of Munich,
Her blondeness under the swimsuit fits
That sunbrowned girl like a tunic,
And in falling light off the limestone island
Fishing boats groove water slick as oil.

Behind them is haze that is sea and sky at once.
In what was the wartime Germans'
Torpedo-boat haven in the Adriatic,
I erase the distinction between
Contemplative and athletic
As I swim, climb out, and smoke. This peacetime weather
Worries me, these seas with blurred horizons.

Stately and wide Croatia, how it shelves
To the waste of the sea, and shapes it!
The silent roadstead shimmers.
As under the narrowed eyes
Of English and German swimmers
Here in the shade, the file of the drifters passes,
We seem much pacified, seem so to ourselves.

Barnsley and District

Judy Sugden! Judy, I made you caper
With rage when I said that the British Fascist
Sheet your father sold was a jolly good paper

And you had agreed and I said, Yes, it holds
Vinegar, and everyone laughed and imagined
The feel of the fish and chips warm in its folds.

That was at Hood Green. Under our feet there shone
The modest view, its slagheaps amethyst
In distance and white walls the sunlight flashed on.

If your father's friends had succeeded, or if I
Had canvassed harder for the Peace Pledge Union,
A world of difference might have leapt to the eye

In a scene like this which shows in fact no change.
That must have been the summer of '39.
I go back sometimes, and find nothing strange –

Short-circuiting of politics engages
The Grammar School masters still. Their bright sixth-formers
     sport
Nuclear Disarmament badges.

And though at Stainborough no bird's-nesting boy
Nor trespasser from the town in a Sunday suit
Nor father twirling a stick can now enjoy

Meeting old Captain Wentworth, who in grey
And ancient tweeds, gun under arm, keen-eyed
And unemployable, would give a gruff Good-day,

His rhododendrons and his laurel hedge
And tussocked acres are no more unkempt
Now that the Hall is a Teachers' Training College.

The parish primary school where a mistress once
Had every little Dissenter stand on the bench
With hands on head, to make him out a dunce;

Black backs of flourmills, wafer-rusted railings
Where I ran and ran from colliers' boys in jerseys,
Wearing a blouse to show my finer feelings –

These still stand. And Bethel and Zion Baptist,
Sootblack on pavements foul with miners' spittle
And late-night spew and violence, persist.

George Arliss was on at the Star, and Janet Gaynor
Billed at the Alhambra, but the warmth
Was no more real then, nor the manners plainer.

And politics has no landscape. The Silesian
Seam crops out in prospects felt as deeply
As any of these, with as much or as little reason.

Right Wing Sympathies

France of the poujadiste!
France of the absurd
Citroëns, still on the roads
Of Marne and Doubs that summer:

Domestic and armoured,
Made out of sheets
Of corrugated iron,
They dive into the highway.

Travelling humps in the road,
Steel-snouted moles,
They gouge at each chug of their tired
Small engines a trench in the tarmac.

Walking is a perpetual
Falling down, and so is
Driving in these shovel-bills
Through the country of Jacques Tati.

Camel's head and hump
Of black rock, Briançon
Bulked not so large
But platypus must nose it

Out, and over ramp
On ramp of France
Snuffle and wheeze
Where Vauban and the Alps

Have framed the camel state,
Its ugly teeth
Yellowed at Italy,
In a geometer's heaven.

His exact nest
Of outwork polygons
Provided parking-lots
For Citroëns in bastion and embrasure

When I was there that summer,
Asking myself to explain
Myself to myself
By enrolling in a party of the Right.

In an old photograph
Dreyfus is falling down
Perpetually between
Two ranks of the backs of riflemen

For treason. But in court
The intellectual
Accuses the accusers. 'Shovel-bill!'
He tells them to their faces. 'Camel-tooth!'

So much I cannot face,
I sweat with those
Arraigned in his
Superb performances.

Hyphens

You remember Rossignano
Solvay, impossible hybrid,
Italian-Belgian? The hyphen
Was stretched to breaking.

Remember its streets, its piazzas?
The main line clove them, rammed
Through a truss of malodorous sidings
By the howling trench of the highway.

Black, smeared on the rocks
In the brilliant mornings,
Pontefract Cakes of naphtha
Stuck to the soles of swimmers.

Mazzimo, draughtsman
For Solvay chemicals,
Shrugging a bulky shoulder
At rigidity of Belgian blueprints,

Dived and hauled up
On the rocks an amphora,
Rough, plain and capacious,
Plucked from a foundered galley.

There too the hyphen stretched
In him to breaking, out of
Maremman cities where his Fiat spun
In week-end pieties

To the Ligurian polluted sea
And unpaved avenue
Which housed him, hardly less
A transient than his summer visitors.

Holding these halves together,
His Tuscan strove
For a coining of new compounds:
Firm-transient, chemical-civic.

A Meeting of Cultures

Iced with a vanilla
Of dead white stone, the Palace
Of Culture is a joke

Or better, a vast villa
In some unimaginable suburb
Of Perm or Minsk.

Ears wave and waggle
Over the poignant Vistula,
Horns of a papery stone.

Not a wedding-cake but its doily!
The Palace of Culture sacks
The centre, the dead centre

Of Europe's centre, Warsaw.
The old town,
Rebuilt, is a clockwork toy.

I walked abroad in it,
Charmed and waylaid
By a nursery joy:

Hansel's and Gretel's city!
Their house of gingerbread
That lately in

Horrific forest glooms
Of Germany
Bared its ferocity

Anew, resumes its gilt
For rocking-horse rooms
In Polish rococo.

Diseased imaginations
Extant in Warsaw's stone
Her air makes sanative.

How could a D.S.O.
Of the desert battles live,
If it were otherwise,

In his wooden cabin
In a country wood
In the heart of Warsaw

As the colonel did, who for
The sake of England took
Pains to be welcoming?

More jokes then. And the wasps humming
Into his lady's jam
That we ate with a spoon

Out in the long grass. Shades,
Russian shades out of old slow novels,
Lengthened the afternoon.

Metals

Behind the hills, from the city of an Etruscan gateway
To the city of a Sienese fortress
Through the metalliferous mountains,
If I had travelled to the age of bronze,
Of gold, the pierced axe-heads of archaic Greece,
This would have been my way.

For first we corkscrewed in a stink of borax
For climbing miles, then under the oakwoods
In unworked lodes lay poisonous zinc and copper.
With forty miles to go, the car bit gravel
Which spurted and hung in the air, and still no houses.

And I saw all stone as a weak concoction of powder,
The golden skin of the columns
Cemented as limply as a Rizla paper.

Rape may be worship. Where the sybil stands
In a pool of spent light at the heart of the mountain at Cumae,
The bowels of earth are of an unearthly weirdness.

Homage to John L. Stephens

There has to be a hero who is not
A predator but South
Of the Border down
Mexico way or wherever else she
Whispers, It's best not to linger.

Fever: bright starlight, and the sails
Flapping against the mast, the ocean
Glass, and the coastline dark,
Irregular, and portentous with volcanoes;
The Great Bear almost upon him, the North Star
Lower than ever, waning as he was waning,

And not that sort of hero, not
Conquistador Aeneas, but a tourist!
Uncoverer of the Maya, John L. Stephens,
Blest after all those beaks and prows and horses.

The Vindication of Jovan Babič

(*Bosnia 1915*)

Age is a pale bird, film of ice on the sea
Where I do not go, film of ice on the river
That I cross no longer after Sclavonian girls;
Cup, horse, kinsman, and the Sultan, the treasure-giver,
Gone from me now. And that old roan,
Lust, is a wryneck since my name was bandied
Among the Austrian matrons and the traders.

I pass for an old lecher since the pear-tree
Under the peeping Tom broke and betrayed us,
Me and my own house-wench. My neck is sprained
Where the boy fell on it. Now one
Of my own house can glory in collusion
With the butchers of Queen Draga, and the hysterical
Schoolboy of Sarajevo. It is a womanish time
That thinks the boudoir is historical,
Love an event. Ideal assignations
Discharge unnatural chastity in wars
Ideally total; virgins' consummations
Cannot be made except with bombs and sabres
And then are bloody. I foresee a time
When all of art and humane learning labours
To clench all history
In a child's fist at the nipple
Or straddle it with four bare legs in bed
And all in metaphor.
    My brutalities
Maimed less, for they were casual, unconsidered.
A flagging wing outsoars them, and the ice
Stiffens the pulse with a not unmanly shudder.

Bolyai, the Geometer

Arthur Allen, when he lived
In rooms beneath my rooms in Trinity,
Thought he had made a breakthrough that would turn
Mathematics inside out again,

As once geometry was spun around
Because the non-Euclidean emerged
Not out of nature, out of nothing extant
But simply as imaginable. Shade,

A flap of blackness folded back upon
Pillar and pediment that afternoon
Encroached upon the chapel portico
And there a wing whirled, flashing. So, I thought,

This turning inside-out is not so hard:
One looks across Front Square and there it is,
A wing that whirls white undersides, sustained
By what endangers it, the press of air.

And though his torque was different, not in nature,
And though my science is as pure as his,
Knowing no revolution more profound
Than that from black on white to white on black

(As though a shutter shot across the mind
One sees the lately formless as most formal,
The stanza most a unit when
Open at both ends, all transition) still

How pure is mathematics? Not enough
For Farkas Bolyai: 'Not geometry
Is altogether pure. This is a wound
Large and perpetual upon my soul.'

So with poetics: never a revolution
But has its mould. Look, in the overturning
Approaching comber, rolling inside out,
A roof of cream moves back through a mounting wall.

After an Accident

I

Smashed, and brought up against
Last things like pines'
Steep shadows and the purple
Hole in my darling's head,

I recall as an amulet
Against my shallowness
Uncalculated kindness
So much! Death, in my dream,

Half-length as in a portrait,
Cocks his eye, leads mine
Up a toothbrush ridge of pines
With an amused complicity

At seeing what is so
Beneath us as a mountain
Tower above us when
We have run out of road.

Death is about my age,
Smiling and dark, clean-shaven.
Behind him the valley-floor
Is ledged in a purple light.

Had I not sought the shade
Of what is so
Beneath us as chagrin,
I had not been afraid

Of his mountainous purple light,
Nor should I have run out
Of the soul of gratitude
Before I ran out of death.

II BETWEEN DEAD AND ALIVE

For you to be thinking how
It was no bad place to lie in,
In this there was nothing morbid;
Nor was it too composed
In me, to think of your dying
As of an emigration.

This century one in five
On that hillside has emigrated,
And this is not melancholy,
Nor the spaciousness disconcerting:
Between the dead and alive
The ratio there is a just one.

And yet I would have sworn
Such thoughts as these were tricks
Of tearful literature;
That thoughts so unresentful
As mine were could not mix
With terror and compunction.

III THE HEARTLAND

And so it is clear that this
Heartland has to be painted
In unrepresentative colours;

That the forests under the mountains
Live in an orange light
Without reference to sunset.

How clear it is, and how
Incapable of being
Foreseen or offered as solace,

That remorse without regret
Is a possible state of the soul,
Like grief without resentment.

IV WINDFALL

So Death is what one day
You have run out of, like
Luck or a bank-balance.
In that case, what is
Coming into it like?

Like coming into money!
The death we run out of is
Not the life we run out of;
The death that we may
With luck come into, is.

And without money, life
Is not worth living.
How did you manage
All these years,
Living and not living?

You never did so much
As when you nearly died;
As if you nearly died
That I might show I lived.

That was no more your motive
Than it could have been my choice.
You cannot think I live
Just to give voice!

It was no poet's need you met,
And now survive,
But the need I had as a man
To know myself alive.

You never did so much
As when you nearly died;
You had to nearly die
For me to know I lived.

The Hardness of Light

'Via Portello,' I wrote,
'The fruity garbage-heaps . . .'
As if someone had read my poems,
Padua eight years later
Is so hot no one sleeps.

But this is a different quarter,
Just off the *autostrada*,
Touched by that wand of transit,
Californian, hopeful . . .
I grow older, harder.

I wake in the night, to rain.
All the old stench released
On the risen night wind carries
Coolness across the city,
Streaming from west to east.

The equivocal breath of change,
In a clatter of sudden slats
Across the room, disturbs me
More than ever, in new
Motels and blocks of flats.

What is this abomination
When a long hot spell is breaking?
Sour smell of my own relief?
The rankness of cooling-off?
Rottenness of forsaking?

I glare. In that renowned
Hard light of burning skies
Nothing grows durable
With age. It neither solves
Nor even simplifies.

Poems of 1962–3

On Not Deserving

Worry hedges my days
Like a roil of thick mist at the edge of a covert
Fringing a tufted meadow. In that field
Monuments of art and sanctity
Arise in turn before
The clouded glass of my eye.
Last year the two churches of St Francis
Were piled up there, at the lowest verge of Assisi.

Autumn Imagined

The shuffle and shudder of Autumn
Are in our love.
Those last thin garments, come
Let's have them off!

Drop them about your knees.
The beech-tree rains its gold.
We are deciduous trees,
And our year grows old.

We cannot procrastinate.
Although we seem to delay
By having children late,
Our Autumn is today.

Indeed, give my body its due,
It read the signs aright
When it trembled at Autumn's hue
On our wedding night.

Hot Hands

'Warm hands, cold heart,' they say; and vice-versa.
    My hands are so hot always
That when they touch your coolness, they immerse
    Hissingly, charred and ablaze.

Folk-wisdom! For such old wives' sullen tales
        If natural law is thwarted,
If a rule of signs, not rule of law, prevails,
        Their sense is not inverted:

That hiss is the first breath I have sharply taken,
        Brought against you. Wrench
The text of the world as they will, they are mistaken.
        I am a brand you quench.

Where Depths are Surfaces

Where depths are surfaces
By the clear Tyrrhenian Sea,
I marvel at life that passes
So clearly over me.

Also I think of him,
The Englishman in me,
Whose skiffs can never skim
That deep, distrusted sea.

His trust is in the plummet.
And I seek equally.
Depths that the lead can come at,
Where all men sway with me.

But boats I would not trust
On the golden skin of the sea
Shadow those waters, thrust
Their ghostly prows at me.

For tides we need not sound through
Flow in the human sea,
Whereas the lead goes down to
Depths, depths endlessly.

Vying

Vying is our trouble;
And a devious vice it is
When we vie in abnegations,
Services, sacrifices.

Not to be devious now
(For perhaps I should not begin
Taking the blame for winning
If this were not how to win),

I assert that such is the case:
I seem to have more resources;
I thrive on enforcing the more
The less naked the force is.

Mutinies, sulks, reprisals
All play into my hand;
To be injured and forgiving
Was one of the roles I planned.

Married to me, you take
The station I command,
As if in a peopled graveyard
Deserted in an upland.

There I, the sexton, battle
Earth that will overturn
Headstones, and rifle tombs,
And spill the tilted urn.

from *The Poems of Doctor Zhivago* (1965):
translations from the Russian of Pasternak

March

The sun works up to a lather,
To a thresh in stupefied lowlands.
Like the chores of a strapping cow-girl,
Spring's busy-ness seethes through the hands.

Snow sinks, anaemia saps it
Along weak, blue, twig-like veins.
But life smokes up from the cowhouse;
Hale, it darts out from the tines of pitchforks.

All these nights, these days and nights!
Thud of the thaw at noon, the spatter
Of icicles dripping from roof-tops,
The sleepless culverts' chatter . . .

Open it all lies, stable and cowshed.
Pigeons peck oat-ears out of snow.
Off the all-blameable, all-engendering
Dunghill the air blows freshly.

Fairy Story

In days of old
Through a fabled land
Rode he amain
Over hill and hollow.

He sped to the fray.
On the dusty plain
Rose up afar
A dark wood in the way.

A keen pang
At the heart griped him:
'Ware of the well-water,
Draw the girth tighter.

173

Nothing list the rider
But made his steed to bound
And flew he amain
To the woody mound.

Turned he at the barrow,
Came into the dry fosse,
Passed he through the glade
And the mount he has crossed.

And strayed by the hollow dell
Come by the dark way
Found he the beasts' trace
And water of the well.

And deaf to the summons sent
No heed to ill bode,
Down to the brink he rode,
Gave to his horse to drink.

★   ★   ★

By the stream a cave's mouth,
Before the cave a ford.
As it were brimstone burning
Flamed in the opening.

Smoke billowed dun-red
His gaze baffled:
With a cry far sped
Sounded the forest.

Thereat upon the cleft
The horseman, ware,
Stepped soft-foot straightly
To whence the voice calling.

Saw then the horseman,
Tightened his lance-hold,
Head of the dragon,
Scales, and the tail coiled.

Ardent from maw spilt
Light showed plain
Three boughtes a damsel round
Wound he her spine.

Body of the serpent
As a whip's lash folds her,
His swayed the neck there
On hers the shoulder.

By that land's usage
Was paid in fee
To the monster of the wood
A captive comely.

Folk of the land
Huts that were theirs
Ransomed by rent paid
Thus to the serpent.

Serpent it was that bound
Hands fast, enwound her,
Took into throes of
The scapegoat the offering.

Looked in supplication
To high heaven the horseman.
Couched for altercation
Clasped he the lance then.

★   ★   ★

Sealed close the eye's lids.
Heights. And the cloud's climb.
Rivers. River-fords. Waters.
The years, the spans of time . . .

Rider, the helm brast,
Brought down in combat,
True steed with hoof-spurn
Tramples the serpent.

Charger next dragon's corse
Heaped on the sandbar,
In a swound the rider,
The damsel stounded.

Sheen of the noon's arch
Azure, dulcet.
What's she? A tsar's child?
Slip of earth? Earl's blood?

Abounding gladness
Flows now in tripled tears,
Now to a dead trance
Lie they in durance.

Charged to new hardihood
Now, and now listless,
Life in the spent blood,
Unstrung the sinews.

Beat still the hearts of them.
Dame first, then man
Strives against cumber,
Fails into slumber.

Sealed close the eye's lids.
Heights. And the cloud's climb.
Rivers. River-fords. Waters.
The years, the spans of time . . .

The Miracle

He fared from Bethany to Jerusalem,
Foreshadowings of affliction weighing on him.

Burrs of brushwood scorched on the steep bluff's oven,
Over the hovel nearby no blown smoke stirred;
Hot breath of the air, and the reedbeds there unmoving,
And on the Dead Sea repose immovably anchored.

With sourness at heart that vied with the sour sea-water
He fared, while behind a few clouds raggedly followed,
Along the dust-choked road to some man's shelter,
Fared to the town, where some He instructed gathered.

And so far sank He, self-absorbed and brooding,
A wormwood smell came up as the field saddened.
All stilled. Alone He midway along was standing,
And the terrain stretched, sheeted in unfeeling.
All swam and merged: the balmy air and the barrens,
The lizards, the gushing springs, the waters running.

A fig-tree rising no great distance off,
Utterly bare of fruit, nothing but leaves and wood,
He said to it: 'Do you do me any good?
Is your stockstillness anything to be glad of?'

'I hunger and thirst, and you – you barrenly flower.
Encountering you is comfortless as granite.
What a trial you are, and how devoid of talent!
Stay as you are to the world's last hour.'

Throughout the tree ran the quake of condemnation,
As the levin-flash along a lightning-rod
Flashed on the fig-tree sudden incineration.

Had leaf and branch and root and stem been granted
One moment's freedom, then the laws of Nature
Had made all haste, and doom been intercepted.
But a miracle is a miracle, a miracle is God.
When we are all at odds it comes upon us
Instantaneous, and when least expected.

Magdalene

People spruce themselves for a party.
Keeping clear of this lot,
I wash down with balm from a bucket
Your feet without spot.

I can't even find the sandals.
Crying, I can't see.
My hair's come down, hanks of it
Hanging over my eyes caul me.

I've clutched your legs into my skirt,
I've sluiced them with tears, and there
I've the beads from my neck for a cord around them, Jesus.
I've smothered them in a burnous of hair.

I see what happens now, each item of it
As if you'd had the whole thing grind to a stop.
Just now I'm so good at predictions
I can see through things, I'm a sybil.

Tomorrow the screen comes down in the temple,
We shall be bunched together at one side
And the earth wavers under our feet.
I've a sense that it's sorry for me.

The escort will form up again in column.
They'll make a start to the movement away of horses.
Like a waterspout in a cyclone, over our heads
The sky will be torn open, round that cross.

I'll hurtle to the ground at the foot of the crucifixion.
I'll be out of my mind, I'll gnaw my lips.
You'd clasp too many, hands that on the cross's
Arms stretch out to the tips.

Who is it for in the world, so much bounty,
So much hurt, such a capacity?
Is there so much of being and life in the world?
So much of colony, of river-run and spinney?

But they'll wear by, three times sun-up to sundown,
And ram such vacancy that through
All that terrific intermission
It's Resurrection I'll be thriving to.

Essex Poems (1969)

Rodez

Northward I came, and knocked in the coated wall
At the door of a low inn scaled like a urinal
With greenish tiles. The door gave, and I came

Home to the stone north, every wynd and snicket
Known to me wherever the flattened cat
Squirmed home to a hole between housewall and paving.

Known! And in the turns of it, no welcome,
No flattery of the beckoned lighted eye
From a Rose of the rose-brick alleys of Toulouse.

Those more than tinsel garlands, more than masks,
Unfading wreaths of ancient summers, I
Sternly cast off. A stern eye is the graceless

Bulk and bruise that at the steep uphill
Confronts me with its drained-of-colour sandstone
Implacably. The Church. It is Good Friday.

Goodbye to the Middle Ages! Although some
Think that I enter them, those centuries
Of monkish superstition, here I leave them

With their true garlands, and their honest masks,
Every fresh flower cast on the porch and trodden,
Raked by the wind at the Church door on this Friday.

Goodbye to all the centuries. There is
No home in them, much as the dip and turn
Of an honest alley charmingly deceive us.

And yet not quite goodbye. Instead almost
Welcome, I said. Bleak equal centuries
Crowded the porch to be deflowered, crowned.

The North Sea

North Sea, Protestant sea,
I have come to live on your shore
In the low countries of England.
      A shallow gulf north-westward
Into the Isle of Ely
And the Soke of Peterborough
Is one long arm of the cold vexed sea of the North.

Having come to this point, I dare say
That every sea of the world
Has its own ambient meaning:
The Mediterranean, archaic, pagan;
The South Atlantic, the Roman Catholic sea.

But somewhere in mid-America
All of this grows tiresome,
The needles waver and point wildly

And then they settle and point
Somewhere on the ridge of the Andes
And the Rocky Mountains
True to the end of the world.

Pacific is the end of the world,
Pacific, peaceful.

And I do not know whether to fear
More in myself my bent to that end or
The vast polyp rising and beckoning,
Christ, grey-green, deep in the sea off Friesland.

July, 1964

I smell a smell of death.
Roethke, who died last year
with whom I drank in London,
wrote the book I am reading;

a friend, of a firm mind,
has died or is dying now,
a telegram informs me;
the wife of a neighbour died
in three quick months of cancer.

Love and art I practise;
they seem to be worth no more
and no less than they were.
The firm mind practised neither.
It practised charity
vocationally and
yet for the most part truly.
Roethke, who practised both,
was slack in his art by the end.

The practise of an art
is to convert all terms
into the terms of art.
By the end of the third stanza
death is a smell no longer;
it is a problem of style.
A man who ought to know me
wrote in a review
my emotional life was meagre.

The Blank of the Wall

after St-J. Perse

The blank of the wall is over against you; which
Is the conjuration into a circle
Of reveries. The image none the less
Emits its cry. An aftertaste of rich
Fats and sauces furs
The teeth your tongue explores
Inside the uneasy head which you have set
Upon the lived with, the familiar
Upholstery of a greasy chair; and yet
You think how clouds move purely on your island,

The green dawn growing lucid on the breast
Of the mysterious waters. And it is
The sweat of exiled juices and
There on the hearth the snapping spar,
Split from how cheap a crate, secretes
The resinous stands of all of Canada.
The need is lived with, that this answers to.

Out of East Anglia

Pacific: in Russian as
In our language
Peaceful is the word
For that last sea at the edge;
And nearer than the Americas'
Awesome, vertical falls
Into the Western Ocean
The imperceptible, tempting
Declivity, inanition!

Sometimes when all this side
Of England seems to hang
Suspenseful on that slide,
How peace might be is near.

January

Arable acres heave
Mud and a few bare trees
Behind St Michael's
Kirby le Soken, where
The pew I share
Promises the vicinity I leave.

Diatribe and
Denunciation, where
I spend my days,

Populous townships, sink
Into the haze that lowers
Over my neighbour's land.

Resignation, oh winter tree
At peace, at peace . . .
Read it what way you will,
A wish that fathers. In a field between
The Sokens, Thorpe and Kirby, stands
A bare Epiphany.

Pietà

Snow-white ray
coal-black earth will
swallow now.
The heaven glows
when twilight has
kissed it, but
your white face
which I kiss now does
not. Be still
acacia boughs,
I talk with my
dead one. We speak
softly. Be still.

The sky is blind
with white
cloud behind
the swooping birds. The
garden lies
round us and
birds in the dead
tree's bare
boughs shut
and open themselves. Be
still, or be
your unstill selves,
birds in the tree.

The wind is
grievous to the willow. The
underside of its
leaves as the wind
compels them is
ashen. Bow
never, nor dance
willow. How can
you bear it? My
head goes back on
my neck fighting
the pain off. Willow
in the wind, share it.

I have to learn
how time can be
passed in public
gardens. There my
dead lies idle. Much
bereaved and sitting
under a sunny wall
old women stare
through me. I
come too soon and
yet at last to
fixity, being alone and
with a crone's pastimes.
In memoriam Douglas Brown

Sunburst

The light wheels and comes in
over the seawall
and the bitten turf
that not only wind has scathed but
all this wheeling and flashing, this
sunburst comes across us.

At Holland on Sea
at an angle from here and
some miles distant
a fisherman reels back blinded,
a walker is sliced in two.
The silver disc came at them
edgewise, seconds ago.

Light that robes us, does it?
Limply, as robes do, moulded
to the frame of Nature? It
has no furious virtue?

The God of Details

after Pasternak

Come rain down words as does
The garden its dried-peel, amber,
Distractedly, profusely,
Yet sparsely, and yet sparsely.
No need to gloss the reason
Why thus punctiliously
In madder and in lemon
Leafage precipitates;

Nor who has moistened quills
And gushed across bare staves
Music on to bookshelves
Sluicing through window-slats;
Who got the rug at the door
Pencilled with small craters,
Sackcloth latticed through with
Poignant, italic tremors.

You ask, who stablishes
That August be a power?
To whom no thing is bauble,
Who goes about to staple
Light leaves to the maple,

187

And since Ecclesiastes
Has never left his station
Working the alabaster?

You ask, who stablishes
That asters taste, and peonies,
Agonies come September?
That the meagre leaf of the broom
From grey of caryatids
Come down upon dank flags of
Infirmaries of the fall?
You ask, who stablishes?

The omnipotent God of details,
The omnipotent God of love,
Whose sexual spark has lit
And fuelled dynasties.
I do not know the riddle
Of the pitch dark past the tomb,
But Life is, as the autumn's
Hush is, a minuteness.

Ezra Pound in Pisa

Excellence is sparse.
I am made of a Japanese mind
Concerning excellence:
However sparred or fierce
The furzy elements,
Let them be but few
And spaciously dispersed,
And excellence appears.

Not beauty. As for beauty,
That is a special thing.
Excellence is what
A man who treads a path
In a prison-yard might string
Together, day by day,
From straws blown in his path
And bits of remembering.

Sun moves, and the shadow moves,
In spare and excellent order;
I too would once repair
Most afternoons to a pierced
Shadow on gravelly ground,
Write at a flaked, green-painted
Table, and scrape my chair
As sun and shade moved round.

Tunstall Forest

Stillness! Down the dripping ride,
    The firebreak avenue
Of Tunstall Forest, at the side
    Of which we sought for you,
You did not come. The soft rain dropped,
    And quiet indeed we found:
No cars but ours, and ours was stopped,
    Rainfall the only sound.

And quiet is a lovely essence;
    Silence is of the tomb,
Austere though happy; but the tense
    Stillness did not come,
The deer did not, although they fed
    Perhaps nearby that day,
The liquid eye and elegant head
    No more than a mile away.

Orford

after Pasternak

With the actual the illusory
With the vegetable growth the granite.

As it might be in Spring on the day of the Annunciation
It is announced to us out of charity
By earth in every fissure of the stone
By a growth of grass from under every wall.

189

By the thrivings of life and verdure,
By the vestiges of antiquity,
By earth in every minute cranny,
By a growth of grass from under every wall;

By earth in every pockmark of the stone
By grass grown up in the warp of every floorboard;

By fragrant thick convolvulus
Through centuries twined over bushes
Twined over greatness gone
And what is to come of beauty;

By the lilac double-hued,
The purple spray and the white,
The various mixed with the steadfast,
Loose sift over the stronghold.

Where people are kin to the elements.
Elements neighbourly to people,
Earth in every hollow of the stone,
Grass growing in advance of every doorway.

Thanks to Industrial Essex

Thanks to industrial Essex,
I have spun on the greasy axis
Of business and sociometrics;
I have come to know the structures
Of public service
As well as I know the doves
Crop-full in mildewed haycocks.
I know that what they merit
Is not scorn, sometimes scorn
And hatred, but sadness really.

Italic on chalky tussocks,
The devious lovely weasel
Snakes through a privileged annex,
An enclave of directors.

Landscapes of supertax
Record a deathful failure
As clearly as the lack
Of a grand or expansively human
Scale to the buildings of Ilford.

The scale of that deprivation
Goes down in no statistics.

Expecting Silence

Whatever is said to be so
Is so, if the saying is
Of an agreeable strictness.

Unutterable until
That way uttered is
What we have lived through lately.

The confidence with which
A man goes off by himself,
Reconciled to a longish silence,

Is not for married people.
Seeds of calamity rain
On our strangulated partings.

Our forebodings say
Much about who we are,
Nothing about the future.

A Winter Landscape near Ely

It is not life being short,
Death certain, that is making
Those faintly coffee-coloured
Gridiron marks on the snow
Or that row of trees heart-breaking.

What stirs us when a curtain
Of ice-hail dashes the window?
It is the wasteness of space
That a man drives wagons into
Or plants his windbreak in.

Spaces stop time from hurting.
Over verst on verst of Russia
Are lime-tree avenues.

A Death in the West

May's, whose mouth was
Open under the gauze.
She lay like a child in her coffin.
Often in that front parlour,
Excessively peremptory,
She struggled to belie
Her timorous nature.

Her sisters found the funds
She lacked, of confidence
To train her for a trade.
Her profession was children's nurse.
Children of conspicuous parents
Grew up under her care
To figure in divorce-scandals.

She and her sister sat
Plumb on grey sands in Cornwall
One day, the two most planted
And stubborn tubs in Nature.
Vivid in pastel sweaters,
We walked along by the cliffs
Over the eye-bright shingle.

She deluded us after all.
If she could not be forceful,
Could she be stolid? She
Liked to sit on the sands,

Looking at wide wet beaches,
Scud over Cornish seas, and
Bright shirts under the cliff.

If one of her ancient charges
Had come in a beach-wrap, stalking,
His tired eyes fierce with gin
From foreign embassies,
Her eyes had been equipped
By so much seaside watching
To know him for Ulysses.

From the New World

for Paul Russell-Gebbett

Old Glory at halfmast
For Adlai Stevenson
Drooped under PepsiCola
Flashing all night on Lima.

There, smiling and contained
And lawless through
The boardrooms of New Spain
Don Felix passed;

Smiling and contained
And lawless through
The boardrooms of New Spain,
He ushered us, and was

One of us. His son
Is at Downside,
His English flawless and
His manners too.

British is what we are.
Once an imperial nation,
Our hands are clean now, empty.
Cause for congratulation.

Plaintive the airs
With sorrows when, sails set
Against miscegenation,
Our keels leaned in from Europe.

Freight of Atlantic airs
When doxies lined the rail;
Songs of the Cavaliers
Twanged on the tainted gales;

The English fever-ships,
Though hopes re-painted, fetched
Up on the Carolinas
To wailing strings.

Rubber-faced Uncle Sam!
Unhappy Adlai,
Dipping in on the clipper to
The heritable blame,

The melancholy strains
No one alive has lived with:
England's historic guilt,
France's, or Spain's.

'What', said our diplomat,
'Sort of nation is
This that I represent
In South America?' I said:

'A nation of theatre-people,
Purveyors, not creators,
Adaptable cyphers, stylists,
Educators, dandies.'

Rubber-faced Uncle Sam!
Unhappy Adlai,
A name that is of Zion . . .
British is what I am.

Zion, a park in Utah.
So many available styles!
Heavens, the New is New
Still, to us quizzical monsters!

Stratford on Avon

I look a long way back
To a house near Stratford.
You had come out of our black
Barnsley, a girl, to Oxford.

Beautiful, boys pursued you.
In dusk and the overgrown
Garden I, as you knew,
Watched you sitting alone

On the creosoted stair
To the girls' dormitory.
No one else was there.
You slept on the first storey.

Lanes crept by the riverside.
We had said Goodnight too soon,
Strange to that countryside
Famous under the moon.

And yet within the echo
Of our lame exchanges
No grasses ceased to grow,
No apple pair turned strangers.

And that was the summer of nineteen
Forty, the war still slack.
Twentyfive summers since then.
I look a long way back.

Barnsley, 1966

Wind-claps of soot and snow
Beat on the Railway Hotel's
Tall round-headed window;
I envy loquacious Wales.

Taciturn is the toast
Hereabouts. Were this Wales,
My father had ruled this roost,
Word-spinner, teller of tales.

If he missed his niche
I am glad of it today.
I should not have liked him rich,
Post-prandial, confident, bawdy.

He was rinsed with this town's dirt
For seventy wind-whipped years,
Chapped lips smiling at hurt,
Eyes running with dirty tears.

A Conditioned Air

A wind I know blows dirt
In and out of the town that I was born in,
The same wind blowing the same dirt in and out,
Coal-dirt, grit. No odorous cloud-cleaving
Typhoon of Crusoe grew upon the West
To satisfy your hunger for afflatus,
Masters of the last
Century, attending
A plaint in the mouth of the hearth, a night of
Wind. The wind
Was a draught in the flue of England. I attend
How the electric motor
Gulps and recovers and
The image on the television screen
Contracts and distends like a reptilian eye,

As somewhere the high wind slaps at a power-line
Out in the country. In the howling quick
Of the bud the branches suffer
Retardations much as you did. I,
Before an empty hearth
In an unfocused house,
Behind me the quietly blasting
Hot-air grille, attend
The delicate movements of
Conditioned airs
I learn to love, as small
As that is, and as prompt
In its dispersed and shaking service. My
Storm-window's foggy polythene claps and billows.

Sylvae

Not deerpark, royal chase,
Forest of Dean, of Windsor,
Not Cranborne, Savernake
Nor Sherwood nor that old
Plantation we can call
New, nor be, it is
So old, misunderstood;
But the primordial oak-wood.

This it is our hedgerows
Preserve from the pre-Saxon:
Not the perennial pastures;
Not Hanoverian georgics;
But a prodigious dapple
Of once uninterrupted
Cover we at best
Subvert by calling 'forest'.

Sprung of this cultured landscape
The fiction-makers of
My race have so completely
Made over it escapes

Nowhere from that old love,
Conniving at reversion
I think of Robin Hood,
The flecked man in my blood.

I think how the tractable Nature
Of the cultivator has
Before now, at the hand
Of many a bookish writer,
Burgeoned in garden-crops
By seasons, and he has
Made homage of them for
Patron or paramour.

But I have kept no gardens,
Am of that vanquished sort,
The gatherers, the most
Primitive of woodland cultures;
I have to offer her
To whom I most would make
Offer, no more than nuts,
Berries, and dubious roots.

Amazonian

Riparian origins . . . did you know
The hammock was an invention
Of Amazonian Indians? Ours
Hangs from a cricket-bat willow
To the hedgerow stump where a wasps' nest sang
Last summer. Out of hands
That could not afford to be feckless it has passed
To us who are
Improvident as primitives. Retted cordage
Rots beaded in
Green light on our overcast garden,
As it might be in Hemingford Abbotts
Beside the sliding Ouse.

Intervals in a Busy Life

'Room for manœuvre,' I say,
'I ask for an undertaking.'
Manœuvring, king-making . . .

Only when death happens
Do I see the tops of the trees
Out of my attic window,

And they are always there:
They have looked on the death of my friend
And on my father's death.

They are the deathly markers;
And thereby, even when leafless,
Green; ungrudging sources

At which, as at holy springs,
One does not drink
Habitually nor lightly.

Filling the intervals
Without propriety
Itself is reverential.

From the New World

Iowa

The blanched tree livid behind
The smaller conifer
Looks to be entangled with it.

Dutch elm disease is in town,
Carried by worms from the eastern seaboard
Twelve hundred miles.

Gesticulating down
And around, emaciated,
This is the many-armed,

This is the elephant-headed
Ganesh of good beginnings,
God of the Hindu, gone sick.

Tomorrow, if the night is warmer,
The snow will be gone in patches
From the clay-spoil hillock.

White on white, a white
Framehouse amid the snow
Is a peculiar beauty.

The tree is an ivory colour.
In a white world there are
So many kinds of white.

They leak into black shadows
Draining them blue. I shall be
Sorry when the world goes piebald.

Red on red was a good chequer,
The red man dead in his blood;
And black on black, the weighed bough swinging

In a night of Alabama. White on white
Is a man of my colour, sick,
Falling down in the snow.

Back of Affluence

That time of the early year
When the sun has a head of hair
Crisp but growing out,
When already the long nights have
Stirred away southward, when
The engraver frost still makes
Likenesses of his sister
Snow, but with a nib
That will not hold its point,

Then the Iowan farmer,
His fodder low, looked out
And saw the prairie white.

He threw up a heavy arm,
He stamped in the house at a loss.
His wife rose lame and stiff.
His children snarled like dogs.

Then he came back with the team;
She into her best dress
Wrinkled at waist and shoulder.
No farming, a day on the town!
Rail depot through to horsepond
And lumberyard, one street.
She with a child in arms;
No place to go from the wind.

Some one has said that it
Brutalized. It did,
That poverty. And what she
Could have seen, she had not
The ease of heart to see:
The sun like a Chinese brush
Writing in delicate shadow
'Tree' on a framehouse front;
The handsomely carpentered boards
Fanned across, splayed over
With a serene springing.

Or, Solitude

A farm boy lost in the snow
Rides his good horse, Madrone,
Through Iowan snows for ever
And is called 'alone'.

Because gone from the land
Are the boys who knew it best
Or best expressed it, gone
To Boston or Out West,

And the breed of the horse Madrone,
With its bronco strain, is strange
To the broken sod of Iowa
That used to be its range,

The metaphysicality
Of poetry, how I need it!
And yet it was for years
What I refused to credit.

More Essex Poems (1964–8)

My Father's Honour

Dim in the glimmering room
Over against my bed . . .
Astonished awake, I held
My breath to see my dead,
My green-eyed, talkative
Dead father come.

That look he has! A rare one
In a vivacious man.
I grasp at the uncommon
Identifiable look,
Reproach. The charge it levels
Is no unfair one.

Hold to that guise, reproach,
Cat's eyes! Eerily glow,
Green, prominent, liquid;
Level the charge, although
I could not have done other,
And this you know.

Hold there, green eyes! But no,
Upon the nebulous ground
His merciful nature cuts
From shot to genial shot,
Indulgent now, as if
In honour bound.

Rain on South-East England

This place is so much
Mauled, I have to think
Others besides these Dutch
And low green counties drink
The summer rains, before
I hold it in my mind
What a soft rain is for:
To ease, flush through, unbind.

Tightly starred, on the flat
Marred ground once, with a thin
Unambitious mat
I mended England's ruin.
Growth these last years works
My roots into the air;
Aspiring on long stalks,
My blooms digest no fare
Coarser than light. The strain
Of self-enhancement frees:
I take no care for the rain,
Soured soil, and shattered trees.

Pentecost

Up and down stairs of the inner ear,
Its ivory chambers, stray
The stumbling, the moving voices;
The self-communers; of whom
It seems hardly to matter
Whether we say that they are
Not at home in our language
Or they are too much at home.

What faculties we are lacking!
We have eyes to see, and we see
Not, sometimes; ears to hear and
Sometimes we hear. But they have
Faculties without organs;
They see and hear with the thorax,
They are eloquent in pidgin.

Our sons and our daughters shall
Prophesy? That gift of tongues
To the Beat and post-Beat poets,
The illiterate apostles,
Is what, if I should cherish
Much or mourn my lack of
Or ape their stammerings,
I must betray myself.

Winter Landscapes

Danger, danger of dying
Gives life in its shadow such riches.
Once I saw or I dreamed
A sunless and urbanized fenland
One Sunday, and swans flying
Among electric cables.

There are so many of us,
Men and swans, in places
Congested with new dangers.
It hurts that we are mortal
Less there, for we remember
Mortal is what the race is.

Swans in unimpeded
Flight above bare hawthorn
Ask, as a more austere
Occasion, a taste for the sparse
That likes its landscapes Northern,
Serener, and more hurtful.

Behind the North Wind

'the Arctic Ocean was open during glacial stages and its
margins would have been habitable for man'

Envisage it: the Atlantic
Cold and silent, ice-sheets
Drawn to the chin of the land-mass
Far southward, but a buzz
Round the rim of the living Arctic.

I fondled a kitten once
Where a blue lake locked in the hills
Winked like cottagers' delph
Behind a forgotten Front
Of 1942.

Empty the iron hills
And the dirt-road to Murmansk,
A cat's nine lives ago;
A rinsing wind from the west
Blew over the firth from Finland.

Will oceanographers set
The Yenisei on fire?
And though a hyperborean
Thesis is revived,
Will the Ob flow backward?

More than ever I need
Places where nothing happened,
Where history is silent,
No Tartar ponies checked, and
Endurance earns repose.

Pages of an atheist journal,
The 'AntiReligioznik',
Scurried on one bald hill-top;
Even the Front up there
Had never moved in years.

Revulsion

Angry and ashamed at
Having not to look,
I have lived constricted
Among occasions
Of nausea, like this book
That I carefully leave on the train.

My strongest feeling all
My life has been,
I recognize, revulsion
From the obscene;
That more than anything
My life-consuming passion.

That so much more reaction
Than action should have swayed
My life and rhymes
Must be the heaviest charge
That can be brought against
Me, or my times.

Oak Openings

The 'I have' poem
(Have been, seen, done)
Is followed by the 'What about it?' poem.
There is plenty new under the sun,
This poem says, but what's
So new about the new?

It is not as if the attention
Steadily encroaches
Upon the encircling dark;
The circle about the torch is
Moving, it opens new
Glades by obscuring old ones.

Twigs crack under foot, as the tread
Changes. The forge-ahead style
Of our earliest ventures flags;
It becomes, as mile follows mile
Inexhaustibly, an exhausted
Wavering trudge, the explorer's.

New Year Wishes for the English

Beware the ball-point lens:
Lord Thomson and Lord Snowden be
Far from your door.

May the girl with the questionnaire
Meet only the neighbourhood zanies;
May she calibrate obsessions.

May the humanitarian
Blackmail be paid no longer;
Instead may you work a little.

May you have, against the incessant
Rain of the new, the all-new,
Indifference as an umbrella.

May you be quiet, may you
Not be hectored by me,
But left alone for a little.

May you recognize that these
Are wishes for the inception
Of a long recuperation;

That they are not what a poet
Would wish you if he could,
But the most he dares to hope for.
(1966)

Preoccupation's Gift

When all my hours are mine,
I husband them with care;
Pre-empted hours are those
    I have to spare.
Step by step, one
Calculated stage
After another, writing
    A laboured page –
Give me my freedom back
And this is how I live,
Frugally, for lack of
    Anything to give
Short of my freedom. Thrift
Gives nothing it gives up;
But absent-minded pourings
    Brim every cup.

The provocations so
Prodigal, and the response
Parsimony? No,
    No vigilance!

The North Sea, in a Snowstorm

Dark ages, calm and merry
Beside the sea of my boyhood
Sparkled on a Whitby
Of cricketers in August.

Blockhouses of 1940
In the undercliff at Walton,
The Roman Empire dying,
A Count of the Saxon Shore
Far from the sparkling synod,
I walk by a sea that is
A concave opal.

Up from its deep, its submarine, sub-zero
Unimaginable furnace,
Rigour arises where it steams and burns
With a superior cold.

Transparencies, and shivers of running greens!

To Certain English Poets

My dears, don't I know? I esteem you more than you think,
    you modest and quietly spoken, you stubborn and
        unpersuaded.
    Your civil dislikes hum over a base that others
    shudder at, as at some infernal cold.
But pits full of smoky flame are sunk in the English Gehenna,
    where suffering souls like ours are bound and planted
    now in the one hot spot, now in another.

The operator is an imagination of Dante
        that plucks us out of the one and plugs us at once in another
        with an obedient pip-pip-pip at the switchboard.
Like you I look with astonished fear and revulsion
        at the gross and bearded, articulate and good-humoured
        Franco-American torso, pinned across
        the plane of human action, twitching and roaring.
Yet a restlessness less than divine comes over us, doesn't it,
            sometimes,
        to string our whole frames, ours also, in scintillant items,
        with an unabashed crackle of intercom and static?
Or will you, contained, still burn with that surly pluck?

Democrats

Four close but several trees, each green, none equal.
They are the glory of this countryside:
Sequestered households of the field and hedge,
Not copses and not spinneys and not groves.

Green and uncertain in the early summer;
Patient endurers down the depth of winter,
Immobile dancers. In these fields the axe
Of the leveller Tarquin trembles, and advances.

Epistle. To Enrique Caracciolo Trejo

(*Essex*)

A shrunken world
Stares from my pages.
What a pellet the authentic is!
My world of poetry,
Enrique, is not large.
Day by day it is smaller.
These poems that you have
Given me, I might
Have made them English once.

Now they are inessential.
The English that I feel in
Fears the inauthentic
Which invades it on all sides
Mortally. The style may die of it,
Die of the fear of it,
Confounding authenticity with essence.

Death, an authentic subject,
Jaime Sabinès has
Dressed with the yew-trees of funereal trope.
It cannot be his fault
If the English that I feel in
Feels itself too poor
Spirited to plant a single cypress.
It is afraid of showing, at the grave-side,
Its incapacity to venerate
Life, or the going of it. These are deaths,
These qualms and horrors shade the ancestral ground.

Sabinès in another
Poem comes down
To the sound of pigeons on a neighbour's tiles,
A manifest of gladness.
Such a descent on clapping wings the English
Contrives to trust
No longer. My own garden
Crawls with a kind of obese
Pigeon from Belgium; they burst through cracking branches
Like frigate-birds.

Still in infested gardens
The year goes round,
A smiling landscape greets returning Spring.
To see what can be said for it, on what
Secure if shallow ground
Of feeling England stands
Unshaken for
Her measure to be taken
Has taken four bad years
Of my life here. And now
I know the ground:

Humiliation, corporate and private,
Not chastens but chastises
This English and this verse.

I cannot abide the new
Absurdities day by day,
The new adulterations.
I relish your condition,
Expatriate! though it be among
A people whose constricted idiom
Cannot embrace the poets you thought to bring them.

Cold Spring in Essex

Small boy in a black hat walks among streaky shadows
Under my window, and I am at ease this morning.
This day reminds me of Budapest. All over
Europe is the North and Protestantism has conquered.

The Roman Catholic North in the black-oak cabinet of
    Antwerp
Is an irreplaceable grace-note, as at Sawston
The manorial chapel of the Huddlestons for the pilgrims.
'Which of them will make a good death?' my friend in
    Antwerp
Wondered through the plateglass over beer and coffee
Looking to the end.
                But I am happy this morning,
Looking into my garden, seeing the cold light standing
Oblique to the grey-green tree-trunks and the grasses,
All over my illimitable future.

Los Angeles Poems (1968–9)

To Helen Keller

Yours was the original freak-out: Samuel Beckett's
mutilated prodigies, for whose
sake these last years we bought so many tickets
and read so many books, were hotter news
when your and Anne Sullivan Macy's iron will,
back in the 'twenties, stooped to vaudeville.

One will, two persons . . . yes, let campus-rebels
account for education at that level,
that give, that take. I wonder if it troubles
our modish masters of sardonic revel
that you, who seemed typecast for it, were not
conscious of Black Comedy in the plot.

You were by force of circumstance, by force
of your afflictions, I suppose, the most
literary person ever was.
No sight nor sound for you was more than a ghost;
and yet because you called each phantom's name,
tame to your paddock chords and colours came.

This too, at this, the mind of our time is appalled.
The Gutenberg era, the era of rhyme, is over.
It's an end to the word-smith now, an end to the Skald,
an end to the erudite, elated rover
threading a fiord of words. Four-letter expletives
are all of that ocean's plankton that still lives.

You, who had not foreseen it, you endured it:
a life that is stripped, stripped down to the naked,
asking what ground it has, what has ensured it.
Your answer was: the language, for whose sake it
seemed worthwhile in Tuscumbia, Alabama,
month after month to grope and croak and stammer.

Christmas Syllabics for a Wife

When I think of you
dying before or
after me, I am
ashamed how little
there is for either
one of us to look
back upon as done
wholly in concert.

We have spent our lives
arming for them. Now
we see they begin
to be over, and
now is it too late
to profit by what
seems to have been a
long preparation?

The certainty that
many have scaped scot-
free or even praised
sets the adrenalin
anger flushing up
through me as often
before, but can we
wait now for justice?

Horace says, Be wise
broach the ripe wine and
carefully decant
it. Now is the time
to measure wishes
by what life has to
give. Not much. So be
from now on greedy.

Idyll

after Giorgio Bassani

As a horn of the high moon veers in clear skies over Main Street
And inflames with a fugitive heat the sea-green pavements,
Out of the town cloaked horsemen ride across sleep
On lukewarm roads that founder halfway in hayfields.

Quiet the night, and clear, and from the moist
Low meadows comes up lightly a milk that billows
In gusts of the wind, and a sound comes of distant trains
Aimed, blindly anxious, at packed market-places.

But you, a god who smiles at the gain and the loss,
Bless your black adepts all the way with spells,
All the good way past fields whose green is here!

The woman who keeps the inn, unbar her window,
Call down to the door the maids from their odorous beds,
Shine in the wine, light rapturous eyes in the shadows!

Brantôme

J'ai eu pitié des autres.
Pas assez.
     (*The Pisan Cantos*)

Burly, provincial France,
Your rarefied, severe
Renaissance is
Material and four-square
Here, in a stout arrangement
Of water, stone and grass
Where the unlettered can
Come and read in the clear
Air of a weeping April
Thus rendered, the austere
Theorems of the jurist
Or fierce geometer.

I walk your foreign turf.
My native tongue was leased
Fawningly, long ago,
To the too long appeased
Long pitied vulgar. I
Speak to myself in French,
Thinking myself in a place
Where a lettered man's remorse
For intellectual pride
And ruthlessness of the mind
May be accepted, not
Pounced on and misapplied.

Looking out from Ferrara

after Giorgio Bassani

It needs there to be no one
Left in the piazza,
Only a boy on his own,
For the thunderhead that shelves
Its far slateblue over small
Lit farms in the plain, to be dealt with
Smilingly; nor is there
Need of more than his hand
Sketching a smudged goodbye,
Before the dark tower edges
Clear of the pinkish mild
Immensity of acres,
Before there be spread abroad
About the roads the darkling
Shade of an old and humble
Townland of that locale,
With, passing across it, the long
Wind of the Spring that will make
Promises some time soon
In whispers, and the drowse
Of boyhood be borne off the meadows
Freighted as high as the evening,
Warm in the wagons the dusky
Grasses, the acrid poppies.

An Oriental Visitor

To a bell in Lincoln Cathedral
A butterfly out of the fens
Of Lindsey has ascended
Up labouring steeps of air
And there, exhausted, it sleeps
Furrily clinging. In
Lincolnshire are no
Fireflies, more's the pity!

Had one of them climbed there, what
Delirious ringing
Over the railway yards
And the level-crossing
And the factories making tractors,
And the minicars at the mini-
Intersections! What
Swing of a coppery rim
To carve off episodes!

To the thunderhead it calls
'Avanti!' – the long high narrow
Pole-pennant carried in rain-squalls.

The spearmen are gone. And for those
With tufted lances, only
The tossing pampas-grass.

The tomb of Atsumari, and
Not one cherry-tree
To stand against it!

When she bites at the acrid
Persimmons of Japan,
It is that from the oldest
Wooden building in the world
A bell begins to clang.

Cloud-treader, breather of mist . . .
A skylark goes up
Into its element, singing.

And as for singing, the
School of the skylark and
The school of the frog dispute.

Meanwhile the one
Pure ring in the world, the moon,
And the numberless stars dispute
The dark green of the heavens.

And the clouds pile
White canvas southward
From where we stand,

And the artery of the town is
A slow-flowing stream between alders,
Though quartering wires criss-cross it.

And though the wintry river
Receives the abandoned dog's
Stiffening cadaver,

Moon-rise at evening; and
An ancient plum-tree drops
This year's first blossom on
A foreign girl's guitar.

'Abbeyforde'

Thirty years unremembered,
Monkey-faced black-bead-silken
Great-aunt I sat across from,
Gaping and apprehensive,
The thought of you suddenly fits.
Across great distances
Clement time brings in its
Amnesties, Aunt Em.

'Abbeyforde': the name
Decyphered stood for Ford
Abbey, in Somerset. There
Your brother's sweetheart Nell,

My grandmother, drew him to her,
Whom later he pitchforked North.
Such dissolutions, Em!
Such fatal distances!

'Keep still feast for ever . . .'
A glow comes up off the page
In which I read of a paschal
Feast of the diaspora
In Italy, in a bad
Time for the Jews, and it is
As if in that tender and sad
Light your face were illumined.

England

I

Eight hours between us, eight
hours by the clock between us,
eleven hours flying time.

Chill and slack as you are,
the torrid is what you affect;
the slipway of greasy Anne
at Shottery launched more keels,
you think, than cleanly Helen.
Although this has to be proved.

A staring world that Engels
never underwrote:
as, of the '45 –
'some few thousand serfs
variously bludgeoned
and misled into fighting
against a few thousand proles.'
The March of the '45 . . .
Confound it, the theme exacted
a certain elevation!

And if there is corruption
in every detail
(notably, of language)
and bed is a display-case
(coloured lights come on:
psychedelic), how
long can the civil servant
at the Ministry of Pensions
remain, as a rule, uncorrupted?

             ★   ★   ★

Heroic fuzz has been
your unparliamentary choice
all over again, I notice.
Hotspur is playing John Ball
all over again. A neutral
tone was (Note the passive
voice) preferred by no one
really, no one at all.

Entranced, my thoughts of you
climb no mountains, enter
no bowels but their track
is outward always and over
a curve of the earth, the night's
selva oscura approaching
and fleeting away beneath me
as I fly over the flattened
Pole or by some other
Great Circle route to London.

History entrances
as on the Great North Road
at Newark for instance, those
bowels we have entered;
but it is less than
visionary, whether
we enter the Edwardian boom
in Balham or Palmer's Green
about the turn of the last
century, or contend for
where Queen Eleanor slept.

Lower to lower-middle
to middle, or else downwards . . .
The drift of any English
conversation or memoir
is less than continental.
I dwell, intensely dwell
on my flying shadow
over the Canadian barrens,
and come to nothing else:
land migrates, and ice,
and Eskimo, and from
his social station my
father in an early
narrative by Wells.

★   ★   ★

Historical time is not
the dimension of these reproaches.
Unkindness is the reproach.
An emptied rectitude
in his cockaded topee
as Governor of the Islands;
a cause of much uncertain
hilarity in 'the Loyals',
in the disloyals, of hatred.
Faithful, knowing the first,
he will not prefer the second.
Unkindness is the reproach.

Sharp? Yes, you are sharp.
The heavy footfall, each
stretch, each stoop an achievement.
Suddenly, disportings!
The younger trees encircle
the thick bole's blossoming autumn.
In the polemical light
between the grey trunks, each
mushy core upheld
still by its cortical
armature of sunlight,
curved knives are out and take it.

I know a man who knows you
so well, so inside-out,
he is appalled by the knowledge;
you must not be seen to be
dishonoured, he thinks, and so he
lowers the threshold of honour;
for your sake he will revise
the entire inheritance downwards.

You are more lovely and
more temperate than you take
any pride in supposing.

Beknighted actors, youth
in tall hats, trailing feathers,
society a congeries of roles . . .
Napoleon was right:
a nation of purveyors.
Now we purvey ourselves.

The amused blade: 'Talk of the gods . . .
you have seen them?'
                    'I have not seen them.'

        ★   ★   ★

II

And this is a poem not about you
but FOR you, for
your delectation, lady;

and turning for now on certain
characters (not heroes,
half my friends are whelmed
in deeper gulphs) who are
dislikeable: Scots on the make
who gave their names to forts
on the Coppermine River or
headlands in Arctic seas.
Donald Smith of Forres
finished up Lord Strathcona
(strath of the coffee-machine?

226

Glen of Conan); and
the Bonaparte of Lachine
(Cathay in French), the bastard
able diminutive George
Simpson was later Sir George,
a small inflexible pin
on which the unwieldy engine
of the Hudson's Bay Company turned,
having eaten his words and worse
for the Proprietors' sakes.

A holy terror. What
a bastard from Loch Broom,
Ross-shire; caught up on McLoughlin
20 days start from York
at River la Biche
July the 26th,
1824
at 7 in the morning. 'Shameful
mismanagement' (forks of Spokane) . . .
'scene of the most wasteful
extravagance . . . high time . . .
ample Field for reform . . .'
'Having performed the voyage
from Hudson's Bay across
to the Northern Pacific Ocean
in 84 days, thereby
gaining 20 days
on any Craft that ever
preceded us.' What a bastard!

Fascist, we have to face it.
No, but I mean, precisely;
not the mere four-letter
objurgation but
a caribou at that
stage of the class-migration.

Nothing to pay, said his kinsman
Thomas, the explorer,
contemptuously sordid,

explaining why distance was
held of little account
'in the North American wilds',
who paid, paid with his blood
for driving his *voyageurs*
cruelly over distance.

George has been blamed for that
implausibly, but still
it gives his quality as
it was discerned. He was thought
ready at need to kill
his kindred if they should
thwart the Company's will.

Or as J. H. Lefroy described him
in 1843:
'the toughest looking old
fellow I ever saw;
on the Egyptian model,
height two diameters or
one of those short square massy
pillars in a country church.'

> (Lefroy, an Army man:
> Victorian rectitude.
> Governor of Tasmania
> later, with the cockaded
> topee and full-dress blues.)

Prizeman of Aberdeen
University, Thomas
Simpson had pretensions:
'The practice of mothers casting
away their female children,
common in Madagascar,
Hindostan, China, and other
countries more blest by nature
than the Mackenzie River . . .';
and sends us to read in Gibbon,
being immune however
from irony. The candid

inquirer, says Thomas, will
also do well to reflect . . .
On what? On there being never
again enough space for our children?
Or are these deeper gulphs
than any with boats or sledges
plumbed by the Romantic
admirer of 'dear Sir Walter',
in 1838
on Great Bear Lake
reading Gibbon and Hume,
Robertson, Shakespeare, Smollett,
Plutarch and dear Sir Walter?

This is the country we fly
over, over the Pole
from Los Angeles to London
or Leningrad. This is where
the Hare Indian squaw or whatever
co-ed from Oregon in
Haight-Ashbury dumps her baby.

Yes, but the driving, the king-
pin, does it have to be Lenin
on whom the unwieldy engine
turns? Is there no arranging
for Thomas Simpson, though
young and vaporous (he
was dead at 32)
to act, but through committee?

driving his crews past Boat
Extreme, Point Turnagain,
and Franklin's farthest?

★   ★   ★

III

The professor is emphatic
when we speak of 'the last eccentrics.'
Bluff stuff. 'Plenty about still!'
He's working at it.

Or there's the unco' guid with
a brutal difference. 'My
father was in the Asquith
tradition, and pro-Boer.
Which is a pity because
                    I wish they'd killed the lot'.
Scotswoman on the make
at 70 plus, where the make
now is, with the teen-age newsmen:
'The qualities she most
values are curiosity,
courage and kindness.' KINDNESS!
Tergiversations of the Left.

The bluff stuff. Double bluff when
back from the Dardanelles
with lead in your lung, Ted Hughes
runs you for a long
still running season, rats
behind the industrial arras
of Mexborough, the pasteboard
Barnsley of grime and phlegm
hawked up, thrillingly mined with
rats and stoical killers.
The bluff stuff. Double bluff.
Brutal manners, brutal
simplifications as
we drag it all down.

Twenty years ago
the gloaming Hamoaze
and the Fal above Penryn
harboured the mothball fleet.
And that seems like the best
time, the point of rest,
an entr'acte of exhaustion
before the impudent flourish
of kettledrum and cornet.
Now some one has said it at last:
Defection! The renegade rats
on a ship not sinking however

but sold downriver to Long Beach,
a floating stage off Long Beach
for What the Butler Saw.

'Display,' said Lawrence, 'of
nothingness. Still, display.
Display! Display! Display!'
Nothing is left of the play
but the character-parts, the charade.

. . . children's voices singing
rou-cou under the drum
of language where the dung-fed
pigeon rhymes with love . . .
When I read the British
contemporaries I
admire, I am abashed
by the levelness of their tone.
They are saying how all children
are, whenever they are
flustered, unkind, however
mild and soaring their voices
under the drum. I have
a reading knowledge of English.

Et ô ces voix d'enfants . . .
those children were as little
children like my own
as doves, doves, are like pigeons!
The words of this age are spoken
from and on a stage.
The speakers are as little
children like my own . . .

Curtain. *Coup de théâtre!*

The stage however is larger
than a floating pier off Long Beach.
It is larger than any one can
occupy. Language envelopes.
It forestalls us always.

Connie Chatterley lives,
or did two years ago.
She asks herself (and gives
an irritated *moue*):
In this extravagant scene
of towering Queens and Queers,
just what is a girl to do?
Or who has whom by the ears
now nothing is overheard?
And what is there left to be seen
by Tom the butler now
we couple like dogs in the yard?

Display! Display! Display!

           ★   ★   ★

IV

England: a Rosciad.
A poem about or for
a superannuated
England, sapped and distracted
by vying rhetorics and
impeccably evenly-toned
social comedies and
Swadlincote, 'so ugly
it made you laugh';
                 and for
Geoff Bond, who came from Sheffield
who died the other day
at 48 and was
ironically bewildered.

(On a Sunday morning he died,
of a pain in his chest he died
within the hour, who had
lowered the threshold of honour
'Why *shouldn't* they swing the lead?' –
to save your honour, England.)

Stromness in Orkney, no,
never; Lyness I knew
in 1942,

232

PQ 17 assembling,
the famous fated convoy.
And I was in the old
'Iron Duke', Beatty's flagship
bottomed in concrete, anchored
for good in Scapa Flow;
and never knew, no more
than Stripey hauled back drunk
from runs ashore, whatever
Athabascan sighs
circle like gulls about
that catchment of recruits
for the traditional routes
through the Canadian wilds:
Knee Lake, Hayes River.
                              Lost
(the historians cannot be trusted)
that long Scandinavian saga.
Sinclairs were of Stromness
or of Pomona; William
Sinclair died at York
Factory, 1818.

In 1831
'Robertson brought his bit
of Brown with him
to the Settlement this spring . . .'
That is to say, his squaw.
And that was Governor Simpson,
got Betsy Sinclair with child,
whose mother had been a Swampy
Cree. The permafrost
spins out a skein of wings
that sting to a sexy heat;
but not Sir Alexander
Mackenzie, whose
buffaloes were attended
by their young, whose elks
would soon exhibit the same
'enlivening circumstance',
who saw Peace River as

'this theatre of nature.'
This is what we pay for:
the language that forestalled them.

The bronze that the poet, naming
his moribund friends, lays claim to
is harder to believe in
now than the Christian heaven.

v

Lay-er of the ocean-cables
from Hampshire, the Anglo-Cuban,
the Anglo-Brazilian, Anglo-
Argentine, none of us young,
in a Manxman's ship on the slant
through the South Atlantic to 'home',
Our Bonny was over the ocean
We sang, not one of us Scottish.

Henry Mackenzie's Athens
of the North . . . My English father's
breeks and glengarry, his
Forth and Holyrood Palace,
Castle and Prince's Street
and Portobello since
1915! Arthur's
Seat swirled in a reek
of sentiment, and along
wynds of his conversation
a Burns's turbid feeling
eddied, a Carlyle's
blurred at the edge.
                              Thom Gunn
played in the overgrown
gardens of Hampstead when
already I wrote a letter
(unpublished) to *Time & Tide*
enthusiastic for
Mihajlovič, that Serb,
Bonny already over
the edge.

234

Browning, Millais,
Huxley, Arnold, Spencer
on the occasion of
Victoria's jubilee had
no tickets for the Abbey;
an eminent actor had,
Thomas Hardy says,
25 tickets sent him.

Shortbread tartans, a voice
for the voiceless and lachrymose English,
our kings implausibly kilted,
we all came out of the author
of *Waverley*. 'Sir Walter
Scott is no more,' wrote George
Simpson, who had not envisaged
a teen-age culture. 'Our
universally admired,
respected fellow-
countryman is gone.'
Gone, gone as the combo
starts in digging the beat
and the girls from the nearest College
of Further Education
spread their excited thighs.

And there shall be no more cakes
nor choruses nor Drambuie
under the Southern Cross.

Envoi

The plane makes travel nothing,
Ann Stanford says, not I.
Thank God it's second nature
Nowadays to fly.
Thank God that 'aviator'
Is now a queer old word,
And every passenger watches
As calmly as a bird,
Seeing the pioneer
Has played his grease-paint role,

Los Angeles to Moscow
By Fairbanks and the Pole.
Thank God to be alive,
Now we can look and learn
Geography through the eye,
And see the cosmos turn
Or the Mackenzie's fingers
Hook out on either hand
To pluck away a mountain
And pucker the anxious land.
Thank God those devil-masks
Of goggles and flaps are gone,
Gone with Hubert Wilkins
And Amy Mollison.
Thank God the histrionic
Temperament must seek
Some other job than flying
To London twice a week.
And we? We can look down
And see, or think we see,
The eider's shank shed feathers
Over the Barents Sea,
And a bewildered freighter
Bound out of Bergen crack
Under the pressure of ice,
Ribs fast-gripped to the smoke-stack.
When in all points like the North,
Lady, unmarked I arise
Across the unwinking ice,
Swilling the seals' blind eyes
With the dome of midnight, think:
I am a rimed unbudging
Mast surveyed by winter;
A sea-mark, yours at last.

Certainly air comes near it;
The idea of air does come
Near to whatever might
Now assuage the spirit.
Air, not the conquest of air
But air, a dimension we have

Polluted of course but that was
Assured by our going there.
(We smell, and leave smells behind us
And poisons, but what do we think
We are, that we should resent
Trailing our noisome remainders?)
Air, the musical crystal . . .
Look, we are buoyed upon it!
As if the Scottish down
Should steer back to the thistle,
Or clouds of pollen come
Intently homing in on
Indigenous British Sea
Starwort or Michaelmas Daisy.

Recent Poems

ICP

Emigrant, to the Receding Shore

for the shade of Herbert Read

The weather of living in an island
That is not an island in the ocean
Crackles in the hallway. What is salt
And ancient in us dries
To an inland heat. The Atlantic
Is a pond sunk in a garden,
A concrete mole has sealed the Aleutian vents
Browned already; only beside New Zealand
Perhaps do sobs refresh
A walled-up bind of waters.

Alfred in Athelney, Hereward in the Isle
Of Ely, learn to go mounted.

Tooling through second-growth Sherwood
In an Armstrong-Siddeley tourer,
Percheron of the 'twenties,
My grandfather unmeaning
Anything but well
Discharged his quiverful:
Aridity, and levels.

The anti-cyclone regions
Of population pressure,
Respondent to the pulse of
Asia, Arabia, Kansas,
Send out their motorized
Hordes, the freely breeding.

And the Age of Chivalry prinks
Pygmy-size to my daughter's
Gymkhana, though the Godolphin
Arabian has invaded
The forested, painfully cleared
Lands of the Clydesdale, the Suffolk
And the Shire horse, the old black English.
The great trees sail the oceans,

Spill acorns on Pitcairn Island.
And all of this is over.

The Break

after Pasternak

Break it off? Listen! we have left a jagged edge,
The whole place is infected.
Sad like this, one might as well be a leper.

Angel, my angel
Of double-talk, don't pretend:
Nobody dies of it. More like
A sort of eczema of the heart, a skin sore as
Your present at parting. What was that for? Why
Unconscionably do you
Kiss as the drops of rain do, and as time
Laughingly kills, for the lot of us, here, before us?

I am so ashamed, it is a weight upon me!
I know, I know, I tell myself, this break
(I made it too soon) it is tangled with illusory hopes.
I was man enough one day, nearly; except I was mixed
With lips and the hollows of your temples and
Eyes, cheeks, shoulders, the palms of your hands.

If I had only, then,
With the whistle of a strophe,
The sign that it makes, and the cry of it, and
That constant thing, my needing you, that young thing, had
    I only
Thrown in all these, they asked only to be committed,
I might have beaten you out of it there and then.
Such a disgrace to me as you are!

★   ★   ★

Take and block me, see if you cannot. Come
                move in upon me, clamp

Down on this bout of my pain
                that crepitates today
                        like mercury in Torricelli's tube.
Move in, move in – warm to it, come, harder!

★   ★   ★

I want to weave together
This choppy welter:
Chill elbows and the magisterial, satin,
Slack palms of your hands, my lady . . .
Bear down on them, arranger
Of regattas! Fast, and take them!
Masts in the ancient forests
In this furious follow give voice,
Fast-gorged with hallooing echoes
In Calydon, where Atalanta
Hounded like a fallow deer
The oblivious Actaeon gladeward;
Where in the illimitable
Blues there was a loving
That whistled in the ears of horses;
A kissing, the insistent
Ululation of the hunt;
And a caress, the trolling of the horn
To the crackle of the trees, of hooves and talons!

★   ★   ★

You thought you could count on distress, with her distended
Pupils, and tears, to be invincible?
In the Mass the murals were going to flake from the vault,
Jolted by some Horatio's lips performing?

This is a drag.
A flagellant is wanting the whip.
Your weeping capes, they might have clawed me home.

★   ★   ★

Amiable, moderate, my own, oh just as, just as at night,
                in mid-passage by air from Bergen to the Pole,
Drifts, lofted and soft, the down
                from the eider's shank lapping like snow,
I swear, my temperate friend, I swear I am nothing loath

When I say to you, 'Forget and fall asleep, my lovely.'
When like the ribs, fast-gripped to the very smoke-stack
                              of a lost barque out of Norway,
Her rimed unbudging masts surveyed by winter,
I rise before your boreal eyes
With jokey talk of 'Sleep, be comforted,'
All in good time, my dear, it will scab over.
                              Be calm then, and no tears.

When in all points like the North
                              past the ultimate habitations,
Unmarked across the Arctic and unwinking ice
With the dome of midnight swilling the seals' blind eyes
I speak up,
          do not rub them. Sleep, forget:
                              It is a nonsense really.

                    ★   ★   ★

Night falls when your head nods.
Everything lies down 'under thy sovran shoulders.'
Switch off the world's light. We have forced the isthmus,

Hand-spanned it, not in flakings! This will do:
The barque in the ice is fixed, the bright privation grips.

Six Epistles to Eva Hesse (1970)

First Epistle

Not, I keep being told, the Time
That gets to me in one straight line
But (I knew this had to come)
A Space-cum-Time continuum;
A field of (wouldn't you know it?) force,
Not that dumb clockwork Time of course –
This and not that I should be writing,
Every one tells me. It's exciting
Stuff, all right (this Time, I mean),
A sort of poet's plasticine;
We get a date wrong – what's the odds?
We're not historians but gods.

Yet some of it seems resistant stuff
Still, and linear enough.
Trade routes like so much knotted string
Stretch out across the charts, and bring
John Jacob Astor, La Pérouse
And Captain Cook into the news
'That stays news,' poetry; in fact
Into geography, the intact
Oregon of their future where
Now in our past they haunt the air,
Faint and limp from long ago.
But although some one says we grow,
If we are poets, like a tree
Through ring on ring of history
Back into our past, instead
Of getting sun to get ahead,
Still, string or insulated wire,
Conducting trade, conducting fire,
Has a sort of truth that brings
Electric saws to redwood rings.
Oilmen and their bankers stage
This very day in Anchorage
Alaska something that no doubt
Time to come will level out . . .

Another string, another knot . . .
It looks like meaning, but it's not.
Instead it's news, and it will stay,
Though not so long as poems may.
Transcending's fine, but then we might
As well get what's transcended right;
No one is going to mount a stair
Planted in what isn't there.
No, Madam, Pound's a splendid poet
But a sucker, and we know it.

Given a set of random pegs –
Five fingers, or a chair's four legs –
You can do a lot with string,
And turn it into anything:
A double helix, say (and that

We know we have to goggle at);
A Manxman's three free-wheeling legs,
Although that asks a lot of pegs;
A swastika; a hammer and
Sickle; or an ampersand.
Come, given fingers deft as Madam's,
I'll outmatch Del Mar or Brooks Adams.

No, look! Unravel it, the thing,
When all is said and done, is string.
Can it, to take an instance, be
Any help, remembering three
Incentives from the Polar North,
The Northmen's three adventures forth
(I'm paraphrasing Olson now)
In the tenth century, and how
His three legs (Manxman, take a bow)
Went West, East, South – can this, I say
Help with that best of Hudson's Bay
Arctic travellers, John Rae?
Norseman from Orkney, was his fate
To come eight centuries too late?
For sanity's sake, what can it mean,
Skipping the centuries between?
Confound it, history . . . we transcend it
Not when we agree to bend it
To this cat's cradle or that theme
But when, I take it, we redeem
This man or that one. La Pérouse
Lives when he's no longer news.

Moreover (it's an obvious point)
Strings webbed from every finger-joint
Mean hands that cannot grasp at all.
('Enslave' 's the meaning of 'enthrall'.)

Thinking along these lines (You see?
We're trapped in linearity),
I'm in a bind, hung up between
The Aesthete and the Philistine.
Now, bind is what cat's-cradlers do
And cradles are suspended too,

And when the wind blows the cradle will fall
And down will come baby, bathwater and all,
And therefore it appears to me
The question has some urgency.
Mum who muttered. 'This place looks
Like Troy-town', didn't know the books
That tell what troy-towns are, nor had
She found it in the *Iliad*.
Contented in her heedlessness,
All she meant was, 'It's a mess';
And that's a sense to which we come
Sooner from 'ruined Ilium'
Than from the eighty-year-old *opus*
Die Trojaburgen Nordeuropas,
Which says the troy-town was a maze
Or labyrinthine dancing-place,
A spiralling of little fosses
Copied in Somerset from Knossos,
Where feet upon the Blackdown Hills
Practised Daedalian rites and skills . . .
– A pretty picture, but suppose
Woodhenge and Stonehenge framed on those,
As nowadays it's thought they may be,
Will that cat's-cradle hold our baby?
I mean, for instance, this Byronic
Writing keeps architectonic
Principles entirely other
Than those so sadly missed by Mother;
Woefully linear, not to say
Rambling. Now, is this a way
To write, from now on quite uncouth,
Not qualified to tell the truth?
Henceforward must a poem twist
Back on itself, or be dismissed?
Or has it as much to do with us,
Constructing towns and epics thus
By spirals round themselves as, say,
Eirik Bloodaxe with John Rae?

Of course it may be said, and should,
That there is no more likelihood

Of worthy characters like Mother
Reading the one poem than the other,
With not much time for either. So
Why not write for those who know
What troy-towns are, and can rehearse
How Woodhenge breathes Projective Verse?
True. And yet one might insist:
What of the biophysicist?
The Muse has better things to do,
We may suppose, than bridge the Two
Cultures, but it wouldn't hurt her
To make her Araby less Deserta.
Will Crick cry, having read Christine
Brooke-Rose, 'Why, this is where I've been
My new-found-land! Arabia felix!
This poem is a double helix'?
Will Watson, spurning from his desk
Anything that's Audenesque,
Exclaim, 'At last I'm catered for!
I like *Piers Plowman* more and more'?

No, but seriously, though
Spirals may make the whole thing go,
The way we got so fast so far
(Boring I know, but there we are)
Must be a linear affair;
Like any track from here to there,
Evolution is a thing
We picture as a length of string.

What irks me, if I have to pin it
Down is, There are no knots in it;
Everything's news, so nothing's news,
And that's bad news for La Pérouse,
Rae, Cook, or any name you choose.
I'm saying, I suppose, that Man
Leaves me cold, though Sid and Stan,
Distinguished individuals, awe me.
(Jonathan Swift said this before me.)
Yet if we hold in one equation,
As types of human adaptation,

The *polis* of Byzantium
And the distinctly separate thumb
(Expedients both to grasp and shape
Experience, beyond the ape);
I mean, if Evolution's not
Over when Man begins to plot
His emergence from his past
(A linear scheme still, first and last);
If, too, it is not Man but some
Named men by whom the breakthroughs come –
Why, then Biology makes shift
To come to terms with me and Swift.
(News, even so, is all we've got;
It looks like meaning, but it's not.)

Teleology, an upright
Darwinian, gave the Church a fright
By saying Nature works towards ends;
'It is *as if* she did,' contends
Teleonomy, his cliff-
Hanging cousin. And 'as if'
(That smart young cousin knows the score!)
Gives us the break we'd waited for.
Thus Comedy – which is all I'm after,
I want to raise no Cain but laughter –
Has raising laughter for its aim,
But aim and end are not the same.
A laying peacefully to rest
Is how one critic has expressed
The end of comedy. (If it's true,
This should be happening to you.)
But 'end', as Aristotle saw,
Implies some things that go before;
Beginnings, middles . . . and those are
Inextricably linear.

Therefore (for now these laughs may tend
Towards their term, if not their end)
I give you meaning, and not news:
Jean François, Comte de la Pérouse,
A person singularly winning.
And to begin with his beginning,

It was in Albi, where a square
(I first made his acquaintance there)
Holds him in effigy. For his
Youth, see the French biographies.
Take him in 1782:
That year his sails lift into view
In Hudson's Bay at Churchill Fort,
Which place he takes – an exploit fraught
(And here see History's comic sense)
With no long-lasting consequence;
But worth remembering, none the less,
For something we may call *finesse*,
And that not least in how he treated,
Civilly, those he had defeated.
To prove the civilizing role
Of France, he next, in 'La Boussole'
With 'L'Astrolabe', sets sail from Brest
To vie with Cook in searching West.
He rounds the Horn and gets his fix
(This is in 1786)
Upon Hawaii. Thence the Count
Makes headway north as far as Mount
St Elias, Alaska; reaches
After that, by pine-fringed beaches
On French leave southwards to survey
The coast as far as Monterey.
After that, Macao and
Manila draw him out, as planned.
A strait is named for him, between
Hokkaido and Sakhalin.
Kamchatka then, Samoa, Tonga,
Botany Bay. And then no longer
The grizzled admiral stems the seas.
He's lost off the New Hebrides.

There, I propose, we let him sleep,
Rocked in the cradle of the deep
Compassionate and comic Muse
Who, smiling, makes for La Pérouse
Friendlier lullabies than sing
Round epic cradles made of string.

Second Epistle

I'm going on with this affair;
Enough of comedy and to spare
In the history of the North
Western fur-trade and so forth . . .
Oh, but you've got there, Olson! Wait,
Miss Hesse, I must interpolate . . .
Olson in a magazine
Explains what his cat's-cradles mean;
Each is, he says, a *trampoline*:
'Trampolines, nets or mattings we
Stand in . . .' It makes sense to me;
His knots in history he intends
That we should take as means towards ends.
The strings of Time are to be plaited
Like woven canvas, bound or matted
Into (these are Olson's glosses)
A vibrant standing-place to toss us
Into who knows what upper air?
(Thus elated, who would care?)
How he bounces! Look how high!
Olson, you're the Malachi
Stilt-jack of our times, all right,
On stilts that spring you out of sight!

Oh yes, I like that. And it's time
I used a Yankee paradigm.
Shall I, I ask myself, desert
Frenchmen and such and, to avert
Any chauvinistic odium,
Lead Charles Olson to the podium?

No. 'Hero' is, however meant,
A title too ambivalent
To give a man whom in the end
I would rather call a friend.
Brief holdings after years of hope . . .
Heroes come dear to those who cope
With the aftermath of crisis
Or shock that follows their demises.

251

Still I confess I have them, clutch
At some I recognize as such . . .
Moreover I'm prepared to find
Their peers in regions of the mind;
Although here too I must confess a
Preference for the adroit successor
Or stout lieutenant over such
Minds as originate too much.
And Comedy suits this predilection;
Plainly, a quizzical inflection
Is always to be heard when she
Presents 'Our hero' to your scrutiny.
So with the man I have in mind;
Protagonist of a modest kind.
And if this paladin I choose
Seems to be French, like La Pérouse,
Why, History upon my plan
Is always a comedian;
And what's more comic than a scene
Where never Frenchman might have been
To plant a fort or write a sonnet,
For all the mark he's left upon it,
Place-names the one persisting, slim
And unpronounceable sign of him?
(I speak of places further South
Than the St Lawrence or its mouth.)
Anyhow, though you'll think this man
French, he is Italian.
Let me present, my verse still jaunty,
Gallicized, Henri de Tonty;
Who earned a fate I cannot choose
But think much worse than La Pérouse
In that, true mate and faithful friend,
He made too late too mild an end
Too quietly. For, like the priest,
The Muse, the Epic Muse at least,
Hopes for an edifying death
And hangs upon our last-drawn breath.
And even Comedy, it's certain,
Likes to ring down a strong last curtain.
(Though Horace taught her she must laud

A Sabine farm, in fact she's bored
With solid worth and modest ease,
Can't see the Bloody Wood for trees;
For we must make it very plain
The Comic Muse is no Plain Jane
And, never quite at home in Boston,
She wasn't always called Jane Austen.)
Moreover – here I interpose
What, like much else, is really prose –
Tonty was, I must relate,
Peculiarly unfortunate:
Geography could not abide him,
Her memorials were denied him.
Backed as he was by the Prince de Conti,
Lake Erie should have been Lac Tonty,
And Fort Niagara was a name
Supplanting on the rolls of fame
Fort Tonty. Thus we see that maps
Fool us as History does, perhaps.
Or else, Geography is more
Sinister than we took her for,
Less the comedian than her sister.
Poets, if they're wise assist her
By calling place (*all* places) holy,
Because it seems she may be slowly
Mustering her enormous forces
To blast her own, and our, resources,
Giving pollution for pollution.
A nice twist, that, to Evolution!
(What's nice about her, to be sure, is
Just that she has such vengeful furies,
Or so a poet may think who fears,
Yet wants, a Justice that inheres.
What will you do, he wants to ask her,
About the gang-rape of Alaska?)

However, Tonty's sun was setting
Some time ago. I keep forgetting.
Turn back the clock, and take the man
Now, at his meridian:
Observe him. Getting little joy

253

Out of the frozen Illinois,
His vigilance does not abate; he
Winters there in 1680
For his visionary chief,
La Salle, gone East, not for relief
But for the needful to equip
There, on the stocks, the half-built ship
That Tonty in that queer dockyard,
The wilderness, is left to guard.
Comes Spring, comes no La Salle. Instead,
Of the gang that Tonty led
(In theory), most decide to skip.
Though landlocked, they abandon ship,
Abandon Tonty, writing thus:
'We're savages, each one of us.'
(A sentiment reverberated
Through Badmen not yet generated,
Who were to take odd satisfaction
In savage pleas for savage action;
A practice copied by their betters –
It has its counterpart in Letters.)
Meanwhile the loyal remnant sought
Refuge and lodging in the fort
Of the assembling Illinois
Indians, whom the Iroquois
(Bless those rhyming Indian nations!
And curst be the exterminations
Of later, more enlightened times
That killed off tribes, and with them rhymes . . .)
Whom, I say, the Iroquois
Decided that they must destroy,
And for good reason, inasmuch
As furs the English and the Dutch
Would pay good guilders for might all
Be sent direct to Montreal,
Should Tonty or La Salle persuade
The Western tribes to ply that trade;
After which brief genuflection
In the economists' direction,
I give you Tonty, some time later,
Trying to play the mediator

Between these rival parties and
In equal peril from each band,
From both of which, to keep his head,
Wounded by one of them, he fled;
And met, in 1681
With no companions but one
Reaching Michilimackinac,
La Salle, on one more journey back.

Now, where Fidelity is the plot,
Comedy, we know, is not
Conspicuously enthusiastic;
She likes her things a bit more drastic
So she can smooth them out at last,
Lothario's peccadilloes past.
Her view is, we are all too human
And stand in need of her *dénouements*,
As by and large we do of course.
It follows Comedy perforce,
When we tell her that we've got
A mystic bond, a true-love knot,
Because her business is untying,
Supposes that we must be lying.
The point is, though, 'Auguste, his friend'
Must get some credit in the end;
And Tragedy and Epic, sold
So totally upon the bold
Unbalanced hero, are askew,
Quite hopeless from this point of view.
So we must make the Comic Muse,
If reluctantly, infuse
The homelier, more homespun virtues
With some quality of *éclat*,
A *Je ne sais* (exactly) *quoi*.
The more so, since we see anew
How History's bits of string won't do;
La Salle's French colony in Texas
Was knotted into no cash-nexus;
Nor did Tonty long enjoy
St Louis of the Illinois,

A place that Kings and History meant
Never should be permanent.
It really seems we'll have to whistle
For a hero, this epistle.
For human virtues cannot earn
The marble plinth, the sculpted urn;
And being trusty, being true,
As Tonty was, will never do.
Like La Pérouse, he had to make
History in a hero's wake,
And drudging on the track of those
Blazers of archipelagos
Means discovering *déjà vu*
Whatever strait one ventures through;
No coral isle, no sea-girt rocks
Not disfigured by the pox.
So, in the speculative seas
That wash up into libraries,
Taint on the breezes of the mind
Points to each Pitcairn that we find.
Thus, as for love of Letters and
Of Arts, it comes, we understand,
From mere debility, a state
That it can only aggravate,
Though suffering's so severe in some
Cases that it has become
Needful, to prevent expiry,
They persist in their enquiry.
(Thus said, as I suppose you know,
The insupportable Rousseau,
In the history of thought
A hero of the direst sort.)

True, there are provinces of Letters
Where these troubles don't beset us;
Regions that Rousseau never knew,
Scrub in his time, now ploughed anew.
Olson hereabouts is found,
Bounding on archaic ground;
And Pound and David Jones are planting
Glyphs with crucial pieces wanting.

Here making a distinction is
Nearly the worst of felonies,
Only exceeded, it appears,
By entertaining clear ideas.
('Cartesian', this crime is called;
A charge at which to stand appalled.)
Here no one's fooled by talk of Hector;
Troy was unspooled, Achilles wrecked her
By running counterclockwise round
The spindle of her Sacred Mound.
Here the surreal is the true,
And hashish may be good for you.
And sure enough, this province is
The nicest of dependencies.
Only, to finance it all
Depends upon the capital
Truth, not soon accumulated:
That zanies should be tolerated.
Now, I concur with those who fear
Truths like this, not crystal-clear
(For crystals take the light, and burn
With furious colours, as they turn)
But plateglass-clear, a sort of glare
Scorching our purchase on despair;
Despair, the bight that we can never
Let Enlightenment dissever,
Considering to what we tend –
The certain term, the dubious end.
And thinking of the poet's (Olson's)
Elastic traverse of the Oceans
And Epochs, how inert appears,
Beside such feats, whatever years
Of sprightly exile taught to Bayle!
That nothing be beyond the pale,
The best enforcement we can find
Is generosity of mind,
Not Toleration's equal haze
Of *plus ça change* . . . (or some such phrase).
Plainly the human lot is bettered
When deviant thinkers go unfettered;
But no one feels exhilarated

At being merely tolerated.
And yet some lump of English clay
Grounds me, and makes me grudge the play
Of mind, the freedom of it. Lean
Limbs upon a trampoline
Of zany theories, crazy rhyme,
Crossings of syncopated Time,
Leap into language. Why I should
Need to distrust such hardihood
Is a question I can face
Best by falling back on race:
How English, trying to make peace,
Reasonably, with Caprice!
(Mercurial Byron was – I'm not
Sure that it helps – of course a Scot,
Where Knox and Calvin keep the screws on
Taut nerves to bounce the Comic Muse on
As rhyming Beppo did. If Byron's
Vulgar pungency should fire one's
Emulation in this way,
One ought to know just what's in play
– Instead of Tolerance and Reason
And all things being good in season,
Byron found, as I find, handy
Rather liberal draughts of brandy.)
And Bayle knew this much: though to diddle
Both sides is easiest from the middle,
Holding the middle ground is harder
And asks more judgment, no less ardour,
Than to espouse exclusive themes
And fly to one of two extremes.
This must be part of what we mean
By talking of a trampoline
Where, yes, no bounce would have a sequel
If tension both ends were not equal.
Therefore the place I should maintain is,
So it seems, among the zanies;
And yet, I don't know how it is,
Tonty and his fidelities . . .
Some more common sense position
Is needed, for their recognition.

So, to resume . . . But why rehearse
What Parkman has, though not in verse,
Recounted nobly? Why go on
About La Salle, son of Rouen,
Or Tonty, his most faithful creature
Whose birthplace was, they say, Gaeta?
Some narrative, and then a moral . . .
With the latter you can quarrel,
And if the former you could spare,
It only comes in here and there.
Tonty should adorn a tale;
If not, it must be I who fail.
But as for pointing morals, why,
The one he prompts is rather dry:
That, pledges being given for keeps,
Whatever just reproach one heaps
(Or might) on fast-cemented love,
Its bargain, though repented of,
Is not aborted by that token;
One's word, once given, 's not unspoken.

Third Epistle

Heroic comedy, I suggest,
Fits American history best;
A charming mode not wholly lost to
Poetry since Ariosto
But, with us, rare. Since being glum
Has failed to bring millennium
At all decypherably to
The New World (or to me and you).
Let's see what being merry can
Do for the American.
Are we downhearted? Yes, we are.
But this is not peculiar;
All of us have been more or less
Bemused by our own wretchedness
Much of the time, it seems to me,
Throughout recorded history.
To raise our moan or raise a laugh,
To blubber or resort to chaff,
Are both all right, so long as we
Can do our thing inventively.

Though gay hysteria in a nation
Seems a wrong sort of adaptation
(This cap fits England, and she'll wear it
With a grin—her 'Grin and bear it'
Is a bore and lacks invention),
Still Comedy, it's my contention,
Can be magnanimous, in the sense
Of showing proper deference
To the pathfinders of our kind,
While soft on those they leave behind.
Indeed, to pay respects while smiling
Is more than usually beguiling,
It may be thought. And now's the time
To venture a Defence of Rhyme;
Rhyme, of all the tricks that are
In the Muse's repertoire
The most irrational, a mere
Foolish indulgence of the ear.
Zaniest of phenomenons,
It makes the rhymed forms open ones –
Open enough to see at once
Tonty the doughty and the dunce,
Or, while revering common sense,
Do it with jokes at her expense.
Is it prejudice to treasure
A zaniness that I can measure
(Sixteen syllables, more or less,
Is the frequency, Miss Hesse)
To random lunacies a man
May feel, but cannot learn to scan?
Total freedom in the fiction
Is of all the worst constriction,
For every licence to surprise
Turns out, in your reader's eyes,
To constitute just one more norm
To which he asks that you conform.
Thus rules we keep and rules we flout
Change places and turn inside out.
And so with rhyme: the Hudibrastic
Form of it's the least elastic,
And what was built as Liberty Hall

Allows few liberties at all.
The licences it thought to profit
By are soon demanded of it;
Surprise! Surprise! our readers cry
And, missing it, lay the volume by.
But rhyme in less licentious mode
Ensures a wavering switchback road
Which, I aver, I trust much more
Than five-lane free-verse highways for
Egotists to roar along
In self-enclosed unmeasured song.
Theirs are the closed forms, theirs the flat
Fiat of synopsis that
Makes every goddess the Great Mother
And women types of one another,
And Hathor, Circe, Aphrodite
One pair of breasts inside one nightie.
That closed-in Kosmos served by myth
Is just what Rhyme must quarrel with.

So, Muse, abandoning these loose
And heated pantheons, peruse
More frigid histories. Tune your rhymes
To Queen Victoria's costive times
When a man could come a cropper
From being in the least improper.
Sing, moreover, in hushed tones,
That most erogenous of zones,
The Arctic, where lascivious day
Whines, summer-long, on Hudson's Bay
And the months-long winters keep
Men abed who cannot sleep.
Thence stiff James Hargrave, terrified
Of waking with a squaw for bride,
Fled, for honour and dear life,
To Bonny Scotland for a wife;
And found one neither he nor I
Would ever want to deify,
For whom I none the less will claim
A sombre record, if not fame –

Letitia, of the Clan Mactavish!
Nature wasnae unco' lavish
Endowing her; not hers the face
Launched ships for Troy or any place,
Though Orkney sailors were to bend
A hawser for her at Gravesend.
Therefore, though less than heavensent,
A suitor was convenient.
So Hargrave comes, and Hargrave woos,
Is liked, and is too good to lose.
This solid man she settles for
Is sixteen years her senior.
And what a settlement it is!
Backed up against immensities
Of muskeg barrens . . . Theirs thenceforth
The Pontine marshes of the North,
Where the swamps and foggy air
Rack the unlucky loyal pair
Through eleven years that see
A due access of progeny;
Five births, one death – one little boy
Sent home, bewildered, to enjoy
The benefits (past computation)
Of Caledonian education.
Her letters home survive, and bore.
Never an item in them for
Revolving Time to trifle with;
Domestic news, too trite for myth,
All on one cheerful-cheerless note –
The baby's colic, her sore throat;
Never a thing that can be pried
Free of the times she lived inside,
The nineteenth century's fifth decade.
Weep, Comedy, to see displayed
The short unsimple annals of
The poor in health: his qualms, his cough,
Her constipation, her confinements,
Her headaches . . . and of all assignments
The Company makes, its northernmost,
Busiest, least salubrious post
Year after year. Who sings the quiet

Martyrs to inappropriate diet,
To wrong and rigid hygiene, and
Dyspepsia in Prince Rupert's Land?
Who ever does can bear to see,
Dry-eyed, the tame small tragedy:
There, on the post they'd waited for,
Snug by Lake Superior,
The cholera descends, and makes
A widower upon the Lake's
Abruptly desolated shore;
She dies in 1854.

Poor child! She comes through as a sort
Of foundling waif, an awed, untaught,
Casually adopted charge
On family estates too large
For more than transient regret
When stewards' households are upset.
Baffled at best, at worst unnerved
By the culture that she served
(The legendary 'Boz', she had
Heard it rumoured, must be mad;
And flagging interest revives
In Shakespeare's romp, 'The Merry Wives
Of Windsor', only when she can
Observe that gentlemanly man,
Prince Albert, showing much good sense
And shyness, in the audience),
How many since have I not seen,
Like her, stand quivering for the Queen
With guilelessness that is construed,
The more the argument's pursued,
As stiff-necked prejudice? Alas,
God Save the Queen from thee, my lass!
God help England, and defend us
All from such obtuse befrienders
As warm Letitia . . . Oh, a cool
Comedian makes her look a fool
Out of her own mouth, soon enough.
Shakespeare, Dickens and such stuff
Possessed, in her days as in these,

Nothing to instruct or please
A hemmed-in way of life like hers;
And yet that way of life recurs
Each generation, with the need
We feel, or think we feel, to breed.

Mothers of the pioneers,
Patching and mending through the years,
Might come to *Lear* or *Little Dorrit*,
Some hallowed text, conceiving for it
Gratitude, as their children had
Proved loyal, or had turned out bad.
But she, who never lived to raise
One of her children, could she praise
Sincerely either version of
The rendings of parental love?
With little meaning and less news
In the record, can the Muse
Even of Comedy maintain
Hers was a life not lived in vain?
Mythographers who can elide
Centuries are not satisfied
Such mournful limits can be placed
On the exercise of taste.
For them, we notice with a shock,
An early death's no stumbling-block;
The racial memory will see
To it, the short-lived can be
Initiate of each mystery
As surely as we others who
Are spared to see the drama through.

Believing that, we might as well
Go the whole hog to Heaven and Hell,
For if blind faith's in order, why,
A crustier pie in clearer sky
Is cooked by an established Church,
Less apt to leave one in the lurch;
As indeed Letitia knew
Who lived and died with Heaven in view.
Sorrowing for her, I begin

Thinking there's some virtue in
A place where prepossessions are
Less confidently saecular
Than where the exegetes romp through
Millennia in an hour or two;
A place where Mrs Hargrave might
Have heard debate she'd think was right
About child-care and sanitation,
Paid holidays and compensation . . .
My native land! secure, humane,
Where no one works (I mean, for gain),
Where, though the rule is Man the Measure,
The module man shall have no leisure
More than an ailing housewife with
Five small children. What price myth
In such a world? What price the lives
Lived there, where computation thrives
To breed the social engineers
Who have the nation by the ears?
Tickets for *Lear* are not much prized
Where all's been de-mythologized,
Nor much of merriment survives
In Windsor's bright unhappy wives
Financing, out of foreign loans,
Welfare and the Rolling Stones.

No, England, if I have to choose,
There are some myths too good to lose;
And if my choice must lie between
Barbara Castle and Christine
Brooke-Rose, I have no wish to flatter
In plumping firmly for the latter.
To be more positive; I bless
All such girls as you, Miss Hesse.
Among the men, too, I prefer
Often the mythographer;
A good companion, erudite
And witty far into the night.
And yet James Hargrave might be more
Welcome as a son-in-law,
Who surely more sincerely grieved

Than livelier men, the more bereaved
In that he was resourceless in
His stolid pain, and could not spin
Tales to himself of passionate
Divorce and death, to cushion it.
I'm glad to leave that thought alone;
It comes, and cuts, too near the bone.

So Comedy, once more our saviour,
Quash such unreserved behaviour.
Do what you can (it isn't much)
To save Letitia from the touch
Of levelling and defiling Time;
Cripple the measure, wrench the rhyme!

Fourth Epistle

Sparkle sparkle, little verse,
Not poetry, nor yet discourse . . .
Let a nation's honour be
Billed as brittle comedy;
Waste and Oblivion stalk the scene
Of *The London Magazine*
And a sickness at the heart
Talk trenchantly of Life and Art.

So, once again . . . But how begin?
Hero I lack, and heroine.
Perhaps a poet . . . Is it time
For self-congratulating rhyme
To honour as established fact
The value of the artefact?
Stoutly to trumpet Art is all
We have, or need, to disenthrall
Any of us from the chains
History loads us with? Such strains,
Wafted on the foetid air,
Are found emollient everywhere
The poet or the painter goes
Except inside the studios
Or garrets that they work in, where,
Though too preoccupied to care,

All of them notice at least two
Sides to the dubious thing they do.
 Savage Landor – there's a poet
Spurned England, and took pains to show it.
Not his the slack, impetuous style
I improvise in all this while;
Headstrong, not headlong, was his case,
Consumed with contumely of race
And insolence of rank, whose sweet
Self-love makes Como seem effete.
 Savage, all too savage Landor,
Less England's Cato than her pandar,
Pimp to her appetite, then as now,
For thinking, 'Holier than thou'.
(Florence was insolent indeed
Not to know the bulldog breed
More than Ghibelline or Guelph
Was a law unto itself.)
No surprise, then, if he's found
In the pantheon of Pound
Who, similarly unabashed,
Was the very thing he lashed:
Ole Uncle Ez, the crustiest sort
Of Yankee at King Arthur's Court.
Both poets, relishing the state
Of mortified expatriate,
Through blunder after patent blunder,
Scrape after scrape, found face to thunder
At home-grown mischiefs, and expose
Fools or knaves, in verse and prose.
 Such doubleness is on the cards
Too plainly, for self-banished bards
Who never lack for occupation,
Each hectoring his relinquished nation
Even as they exemplify
The prepossessions they decry.

Besides, we've reached rock-bottom now;
Byronic skiff and Crabbe-like scow
And Landor's lovely craft alike,
Forced upon the shoreline, strike.

They fill before they feel the shock,
In such small print it is; the rock
Of the obituaries, on whose
Shallow ubiquity the Muse
Time and again has struck and foundered.
The insignificant! The unsounded
Reaches of the trite! We grind
The lakebed gravels of the mind.
A stilted posy on the grave
Is all that Art can do to save
Poetry's and a Nation's honour:
'Canada's soil lie light upon her . . .'
As upon so many others,
Sickly brides, benighted mothers,
French explorers. Only places,
Patches of earth, by the good graces
Of local polymaths sometimes
Name, to make exotic rhymes,
Small successes or near-failures:
Ill-bred wives, unlucky sailors.
        Thus New Zealanders maintain
The name of Marion du Fresne
Who, Skye-ward navigating, tore a
Princely botanist from his Flora
Once upon a time; who now
Knows better than to make his bow
To a no longer Young Pretender.
Instead he dwells in modest splendour
On a colonial estate
Secured in 1768
In l'Île de France (which is to say
Mauritius, at the present day).
        And yet he rushes on his doom,
Sets all at risk, and will resume
Nautical life. He sinks behind
The south-east skyline, there to find
Some paltry islands, of which one
Commemorates him: Marion
His mark, his sea-mark. (And this matters
Astringent comedy never flatters
The ruinous Quixotes of their day,

John Franklin or Wolfe Tone or Che,
Too virginal to wed Success,
Intact in ineffectiveness.)
Not Carthaginian Hanno nor
Odysseus, prudently inshore,
Their crude technologies unripe
For the deep waters, is his type;
The mythological parallel
As usual works out far from well
As soon as we imagine how
Things really were. Take notice now,
For instance, that the second ship,
Manœuvred with poor seamanship,
Hereabouts with some commotion
Collides with his one in mid-ocean;
The culprit turning out to be
A sprig of the nobility,
The mishap cannot help but seem
Due to the *ancien régime*,
A far from mythical condition
Through which he limps upon his mission,
Hurrying now, and making for
Tasmania's vaguely charted shore
There to recoup, refit. But no,
Van Diemen Land cannot bestow
Wood, nor water, nor much ease
Not vexed by aborigines.
      In March of 1772,
Accordingly, he ploughs the blue
Waters of the Tasman Sea
Helped by a strong south-westerly,
Makes land and, weathering new mischances,
Declares New Zealand thenceforth France's.
North Island's earth lie light upon
The breast *etcetera* of one
Whose bones, outlandish treasure-trove,
Enrich Assassination Cove.
(That is to say, his bones at least;
His meat had made a Maori feast.
Comedy goes for jokes like these;
Her humour's black, like Cruelty's.

Unamiable! None the less,
Noteworthy for straightforwardness:
If in such rites she shows us how
To be as crude as Chairman Mao,
Cruelty's what she had in mind;
She won't be cruel to be kind
Nor, anthropophagous, pretend
Doing it serves some higher end.)
       From Utopian projectors
Caustic Comedy protect us!
Under whose corrosive shield
I re-affirm we ought to yield
Firm pre-eminence of status
Among projections, to Mercator's;
Trusting the lie of lands and seas
Before such lies as History's.
       Between his stanchions I can sling
My own small lattices of string,
Slack hammocks where I can compose
Into a somnolent repose
The harrowing abbreviations
Of lives endured, inured to patience
Or insensate, flailing round
Some misappropriated ground
Of pride or Polynesia or
That atoll not worth sailing for,
National honour. Lulled upon
The loll of reverie, even one
That time was at no pains to ravish –
Letitia Hargrave, born Mactavish,
Raped in her own and History's sleep –
Is comforted and learns to keep
Good company in the Isle of Skye,
The Bay of Islands and Versailles.
The dancing clews, the bulk and sway
Of slipping shadows web the day
Between decks to the music of
Strains and chafings, suave enough
To help us orchestrate a mood
By latitude and longitude;
Parameters our captains must

Abstractedly pursue and trust,
And by their grid upon the chart
Mesh fluid Nature into Art,
But which, in truth, will barely serve
To plot our conquest of the curve
Of oceanic earth. Instead
We can weave a swinging bed
(Too lax to make a trampoline)
Of the surprising, unforeseen
Conjunctions human beings prove
The more the rule, the more they move.

Most poets sail another tack:
To the Piraeus, and then back.
Browning's anxiously despairing
Enquiry, 'What's become of Waring?'
Asked of one who took his chance
In poor Marion's Austral France,
Still touchingly pursues us where
We've emigrated to, by air.
And Landor, Pound and Browning are
All in this sense too insular
To help us much, who need to probe
A way to humanize the globe
By which (upon this point I yield)
Space and Time inscribe one field,
But (and here I give no quarter)
Space is the long side, Time the shorter.

Still, older poets had the sense
At least to run a staked-out fence
Around their fields. And those fields are
Better than rectilinear;
The curve of earth takes care of that,
Unless of course you think it's flat
As apparently those do
Whose pastures melt into the blue
Unfenced Beyond of the sublime,
The mythopoeic waste of Time.
     True, the power of myth engages
Some of the old masters' pages.

(They know things are not what they seem;
That in the Polynesian scheme
Of things it may be Marion died,
A case of ritual deicide.)
But La Pérouse's rigid page
Is icy with contempt and rage,
Telling the not dissimilar end
Of his own too trusting friend,
De Langle, butchered out of reach
Of help on a Samoan beach;
Unfair it may be, but I fear
(Miss Hesse or any other dear
Reader) those bluff sailors thought
Ill of people of our sort
Whose surveys, something less than global,
Had declared the savage, noble,
Thereby fashioning a myth
Their shipmates could be murdered with.

Fifth Epistle

A thesis, though sincerely meant
Is in the end impertinent,
Comedy says. In her sharp praxis
There's no place for grinding axes;
Thesis, antithesis, the same,
A more or less convenient frame
For weaving on. The web is tattered;
Mending it's all that ever mattered.
        All the same, an axe is ground
So gratingly, on that renowned
Marmoreal paragon, Captain Cook,
Its squeak is hard to overlook.
Was it presumption when he trod
Hawaii, an acknowledged god?
Did, when he died, the Age of Reason
Learn the irrational was in season?
There, on the black sand, hacked, dismembered
Worshipfully, he remembered,
Did he, that last instant, how
A man-god could not disavow
In Gethsemane the weight

Of divinity, and fate?
Or did he, dying blindly, still
Think that, given mind and will,
Something there was a man could do
To exorcise a myth come true?

A worse hypothesis will fit him:
That he never knew what hit him.
Navigator through and through,
Hydrographer with a job to do,
Was that James Cook? The very first
(So Coleridge was to say) that burst
Into that silent sickening sea –
Professional speciality?
– A mask, perhaps; the shy, self-made
Provincial hides behind his trade.
If so, it works: the self-respecting
Yorkshireman there's no detecting.
In the Ridings we admire
The man with expertise for hire,
Who by his code austerely sells
Fierce competence, and nothing else.
Wilfrid Rhodes and Maurice Leyland
And Hedley Verity . . . I stand
Dwarfed by Father as we clap,
And surly Leyland tugs his cap
And (No, this *isn't* out of books)
Black as Lucifer he looks,
Coming with a racing stride
And booted thunder, past our side
Up the pavilion steps, to gain
His private dark. Aye, Bramall Lane
Will never see his like again . . .
And just as well – it was a poor
Cramped nobility, to be sure,
That disdainful dourness which
Had the globe for cricket-pitch
Once – which now, if it survives
At all, informs the sullen lives
Of Yorkshire bards who take perverse
Pride in writing metred verse,

All their hopes invested in
One patent, brilliant discipline.

Well, we can hardly pick and choose:
Not much to gain, but much to lose,
We find nobility where we can,
Even in a Yorkshireman.
But that is neither here nor there;
Nobility's not comic fare.
Nor are cowards – which puts paid
To the horribly afraid
Lieutenant Williamson. Nor is
The brave and brutal Bligh, whose story's
Never been told with justice, such
A theme as Thalia's light touch
Does justice to. And so we might
Scan all whom History's brought to light
Out of the muster of Cook's two
Ships and, having conned them through,
Rule the lot of them out of court.
(Our Muse is choosier than we thought.)
Instead, as you'll have guessed, there's one
Case that I've chosen – Corporal John
Ledyard.
            He's been much maligned,
Ledyard has, by those who find
Any disrespect for Cook
A hanging matter, in their book.
(Whereas, for Cook's own sake, in fact
Blemishes is what we've lacked
All this while, and any stain
Of fallibility's sheer gain.)
And Ledyard, on the other hand,
Though seldom in his native land
Remembered, was a curious man,
Authentic and American.
In 1787 he strode
Along his own untravelled road
In winter, carrying all he had,
From Stockholm round to Petrograd,
1200 miles on foot in eight

Weeks . . . But I anticipate:
Some years before, with Cook, he'd been
A less accomplished peregrine;
As witness his account of it,
Where passages of exquisite
Silliness reveal a man
Whose role, not yet pedestrian,
Is never to be much surprised
When sudden gusts of bowdlerized
Laurence Sterne (from whom he's stealing)
Type him as the Man of Feeling.
(Words! Insidious avengers!
Time, that brings in its revenges,
Has too keen, too true an ear:
It's not enough to be sincere,
You have to seem so. History smiles,
Custodian of exploded styles.)
'Mystic sheer distance was in thine
Eye,' wrote Olson's friend and mine,
Ed Dorn, addressing Ledyard. And
'Mystic' is right. It was the land,
Dorn's land and his, made manifest
In him its destiny, heading West
The long way round if need be, by
Tomsk and Kachuga. 'In thine eye',
Ledyard, all America smiles
Already, ribboning through miles
Of trailers, and the pent air slaps
Whick-whick against us through the gaps
Between the parked cars, as we prove
The way to live is on the move.

To wrest from Russia the distinction
Of slaughtering into extinction
Such animals as Steller's sea-
Cow and the sea-otter, he
(So the accepted version goes)
Had the prescience to propose
America dispute the ground
The Russians had, from Nootka Sound,
And thus imperiously invade

The fortune-making peltry trade
That desolated Arctic seas
To warm the backs of Cantonese.
And there's his greatness! What a man
It took, to frame so gross a plan!
What a Napoleon of crime,
Born not before, but of, his time!
Thus the historians, lost in awe
As soon as Nature's rule of law
Is breached on a sufficient scale.
Cachalot and walrus quail.
Prayed after from Connecticut,
Dissolute grave whalers gut
Leviathan's cows, and under Cape
Brett in the Bay of Islands rape
Maori women on the sands
Mauled by Marion's dying hands.

Luckily, none of this is true:
Any nation's flag would do
To plant upon the unexplored,
Unbestowable seaboard
That beckoned Ledyard like a dream,
Unprofitable and extreme.
America and Freedom earn,
It's true, apostrophes *à la* Sterne
Still, in the desultory pages
That trace him by Siberian stages
Eastward; but after John Paul Jones
And Jefferson fail to raise the loans
He'd hoped to touch them for, occurs
No mention of the trade in furs.
A pretext that had failed to raise
The wind, he might as well erase
(And did) from the aspiring mind
That thought to benefit mankind . . .
Travelling as sheer condition!
Exploring *that* was the commission,
Self-bestowed, on which he went
Walking through a continent.
Thus was History outwitted!

He wore the motley till it fitted;
The reach-me-down of silly phrases,
Exclamation marks, self-praises,
Points and frills, falls into shape.
Can mere farrago thus escape
The times' and Comedy's clutching hands?
Yes. When Catherine countermands
Her passe-partout, and by her order
He's dumped across the Polish border,
No one has the heart to smile
At the pretensions of his style.
Deluded, verminous, alone,
The rhetoric he'd made his own
Comes true, at last his situation
Demands the note of desperation.
His fever-pitch was queered before
The Empress pushed him out the door.
Febrile, excitable, effusive
He chose to be, and chose to live
Up to what that style demands,
Grasping his fate with shaking hands.

And so he fades from us, you see . . .
A figure, once, of comedy,
Now asking for some other kind
Of honorarium, gone to find
Death in Cairo in the very
Year that saw his plans miscarry
Of following a Yankee star
Through the dominions of the Czar.
(I'm sorry, by the way – and yet
It's fitting, when you think of it –
That I couldn't follow through
The life of Ledyard with the due
Observance of successive time
That Comedy exacts of rhyme;
I trust that none the less you've pieced
Together, bit by bit, at least
A general notion where he went
First and last, and in the event
With what success.) There still remains

One awkward truth: for all the pains
We take at Comedy's behest
To be poised and unimpressed
And keep our heads, we cannot guard
Against, nor take account of, hard
Gamblers of the do-or-die
Variety, who make the sky
Their limit, and provoke their fate
By being disproportionate.
Comedy just cannot brook
A Ledyard, nor perhaps a Cook . . .
So, dear Miss Hesse, if I were you
And you were found to be the true
Empress Eva of all Russia,
Faced with a Ledyard, I should usher
Him out across my frontier fast;
Heroes are safest in the past.

Sixth Epistle

The impetus, awesome!
The imperial momentum
Flogs still: 'Among the first
And farthest . . .' The unslakeable thirst
Still logs its marches. If it is
Late for these intensities,
If it's too late (or else too soon)
For landing parties on the moon,
Then ponder an alternative:
That fever, easier to forgive,
When a Ruskin's narrowed eyes
Crimp to the nicer enterprise,
'Not place, but the expression on
The face of it.' The light is gone
Over the lake and off it, while
Autumn, the amber of a style,
Dyes it his in whom his own
Time and the year's time mix a tone
Mellowed for it. And for this
Meshing of uncertainties
Not too late? The space for it
Is narrowed on the face of it,

Branded with a coming doom
Wreaked or suffered. Little room
Left to articulate the fine
Crowsfoot and serif, scroll and line,
When Nature's indeterminate face
Frowns, or fawns with craven grace
On her despoiler. Still, it is
An honourable emphasis –
On the refining mutual shock
When ravisher and patient lock
Looks in one haggardness that hones
Weasel and rabbit to thin bones,
To one bleached gossamer. The tension
Of a mortal apprehension
Steadies the web to such a fine
Reticule, the debile line
Parts at the pressure of a gnat.
No cradle here, to swing a cat!

Says Romance: 'You need some rope.
Put away your microscope,
Set your manikin in motion
Across what continent or what ocean
All you need's a general notion.'
Insufferable! If it's true
There's virtue in a bird's eye view,
Some better reason must be found,
Still valid when we're on the ground.
It might be this: that there is one
Abstracted potent lexicon
Of place, which helps us understand
Where, in some ultimate sense, we stand;
That heath and strand and wood and cape
Make up a grid we can't escape,
However manifestly these
Vary with localities.
And being English helps with this.
My emblem of all barrens is
The Langsett moors, and the Great Wood
Is tiny Hugsett, where we would
Cull bluebells forty years ago:

Great Wood, Great Barrens, though we know
Better, or worse. Thus 'great' and 'far',
'Remote' and 'wild' and 'trackless' are
Nomenclature that cannot fail
To stay authentic and in scale,
Being as felt. We made our claim
To them, for instance, with the name
'North America' for the last
Ruined homestead that we passed
Breasting the moor. Domesticated
Little England is, and fated
To get much more so; none the less
This way she'll march with Lyonnesse
For us, for good. And Lyonnesse
Or Tryermaine is wilderness,
Bewildering, and not lightly entered,
Where if we travel (as demented
Aberrant Ledyard punned) we are
In error. There, the near is far,
The old home unfamiliar,
The little, great. But all the same
Great this, great that, advance a claim
By authors of an island-nation
That demands substantiation,
For instance, as to climate. Why
Should we suppose a scudding sky
And chill damp airs delineate
More truly than less temperate
Weathers do, our mortal state?
Moreover, 'manikin' may do
For hobbits or an elf or two
Or for myself when, still a child,
I took for emblem of the wild
And waste, a meadow rank with clover
And vetches, long ago built over.
But Geography's too great
And fierce a power to tolerate
Being, through a Tolkien's eyes,
Toyed with, and cut down to size.
    It may well be that any scene
On land or water, whether seen

Up close or from a long way off,
Presents us with at best a rough
Approximation to the true.
And yet the snail's, the bird's eye view
Both serve us better, we may hope,
Than turning round the telescope
Until what's insular and near
Seems crisp, definitive and clear
As in Romance. Romance, though charming.
Seeming gratuitous and disarming,
Has in fact an end in view
Not always good for me or you.

Therefore, like others we've applauded,
Our final actor's a recorded
Personage – the most renowned
Hero in fact I've so far found:
Thomas Jefferson!
                        My reader,
Though he's British, shouldn't need a
Résumé of *that* career.
But every one will think it queer
If I propose him as a prime
Example, in his place and time,
Of the comic. So he seems,
However, if the several themes
I've tried to tease out in this poem
Have any rhyme or reason to 'em.
Indulgent friends like you, Miss Hesse,
Will take my drift. Let others, less
Persuaded or amused, reflect
That Comedy is circumspect;
So statesmanlike that a Romantic
Pathos winces at each antic
She performs upon the stage
Of Jefferson's or any age.
Comedy always keeps her cool
When other Muses play the fool.

The curtain rises! There, before us,
Stands a patron of explorers:

Ledyard and Meriwether Lewis.
Difficult deciding who is
The crazier of that couple. He,
Sincere in his civility,
Dispatches to their destinations
Both of them, their aberrations
Noted, allowed for. When they die,
Both violently, in his eye
Brightens a pained, regretful smile
As he, in one unruffled style
(Too humane a style to break,
Too inclusive to mistake
For mischance, logic) with entire
Justice, in the steady fire
Of rational prudence immolates
Both in one memoir. In their fates
He reads excess, and so impales
The pair of them. He never fails.
. . . As does, for instance (I regret
Digging a little deeper yet
Into Americana) his
One-time foil in rivalries
For President, the first John Adams.
The only rhyme to that is 'madam's'
As Yeats discovered; so it's yours,
Miss Hesse, who will recall of course
Among the Adamses, that Brooks
Whose wayward, dazzling history-books
Are monotonously found
Scriptural, by Ezra Pound.
And, reader, this is no digression:
Brooks comes of John, by due succession,
And Henry too . . . in all we see
Men mesmerized by History.
Set Jefferson against his peer,
Adams, and the issue's clear –
The one, successful and serene;
Behind him mountains; and between
His sanguine forehead and the rim
Of the medal struck for him,
Stretching savannahs: but behind

The other's angry head, designed
By an engraver in the pay
Of secret party, some *mêlée*
Or massacre or mob-unrest,
A tumult of crossed interest,
Crowding the middle ground inside
The milled edge of resentful pride.

Of course we know which one we like:
Betrayed, traduced, and with the strike
Against him always, Adams. Yet
It's Jefferson we can't forget
Who, though he never went there, hung
All Oregon upon a young
And urgent nation's parlour-wall.
Our hearts go out to those who fall,
Success is vulgar. None the less
A breakthrough into spaciousness,
New reaches charted for the mind,
Is solid service to mankind.

Trevenen

I

His Return (Christmas, 1780)

Winds from Cook's Strait cannot blow
Hard enough to lift the snow
Already comfortably deep
Where Roseveare and Treyarnon sleep;
Knit to the centre from the far
Fastness of their peninsula,
The Cornish dream that distance can
Deliver their young gentleman
Unaltered to his mother's arms,
To be in rectories and farms,
Assembly-rooms and markets, shown
As the great Cook's and yet their own.
        Camborne's as certain as St James
That vocabulary tames
The most outlandish latitude;

That, at a pinch, to speak of rude
Hardihood will meet the case
And teach a Bligh to know his place;
And 'gallant' and 'ingenious' will
Confine their irrepressible
Midshipman who murders sleep,
Sprung from the London coach to heap
His hero-worship of the dead
Hero on each doting head.
     It would be years before he knew
Himself what it had brought him to;
What it had meant, his profiting
By the good offices of King
And Bligh, the mote-dance in the air
Of their vacated cabins where
Sea-glitters pulsed above his head
Bent to his books. And loving dread
Of his commander's furies taught
Lessons of another sort
If he could trust to having seen
How far from rational and serene
Command might be. When, at the oar
Under Cook's marginally more
Indulgent but still beetling eye,
He clawed a cutter round the high
Northwestern overhang, it meant
The profile of a continent.
So much he knew, and knew with pride;
And yet he was not satisfied,
Not now, nor later. But for now
He chatters to his mother how
Captain King he can instate
As the dead Cook's surrogate:
King, with his connections; King
In Ireland now and finishing
The narrative of the fatal cruise
(Awaited, though no longer news);
King, and his kindness (Bligh, the spurned,
Unconnected patron, burned
With a jealousy that seared
King's account, when it appeared,

With marginalia . . .); King, whose eyes
Smiled on skill and enterprise
Such as young Trevenen knew
He could boast, and ardour too;
Sweet James King, whom more than one
Hawaiian wanted for a son;
King, then (and so the plaudits end)
At once a mentor and a friend,
Rare composite of gall and balm,
Skilful to command and charm.

      Thus, mixed with talk of azimuth
And quadrant, to confound Redruth,
Trevenen, merrily enough,
Talks of how it merits love,
Some men's authority; and some
Clerical auditors keep mum,
Shocked to know how near they come
To greeting (so enthralled they are)
With an impious 'huzzah'
Such a sublime condition as
They've pressed on their parishioners
As more than human. 'Well, but no,'
They tell themselves, 'the boy don't know
How near he grazes Gospel-truth.
Brave spirit of ingenuous youth!'
And so they huff and puff it home
With (to their wives) 'Come, madam, come!'
Their wives and daughters half aware
Dear Papa has an absent air.

      It troubles him, as well it might,
To see in such resplendent light
Mortal redeemers crowd upon
A stage that should be cleared for One,
That One, Divine. There was some doubt
Whether Cook had been devout;
Though as to that one could not feel
Happy with excess of zeal,
Remembering saintly Wesley whose
Vexatiousness had emptied pews
Down all the stolid Duchy, packed
Gwennap Pit, and loosed in fact

Who knew what furies in deluded
Tin-mine Messiahs? So he brooded,
The honest rector. As for that,
He thought, there's worse to wonder at:
Wrong principles inflame and spread
When they aureole a head
Rank has exalted more than those
Who merely by their talents rose.
Thus, nothing's more alarming than
That too warm Christian gentleman,
Lord George Gordon, the inspired
And loved authority that fired
Prison and church, and did not spare
Lord Mansfield's house in Bloomsbury Square . . .
'Bah!' he thought, 'what has all this
To do with young men's loyalties?'

II

Life and Contacts (1784–7)

The poet Crabbe, with whom he shared
Burke as patron, never cared
(It appears) to throw a frame
Round the poems that made his fame.
There, as if through window-glass,
Men like James Trevenen pass
Plain and unflattered. Never mind
Asking what poetic kind
Crabbe's tales belong to; they escape
Any predetermined shape,
Comic, heroic, or whatever.
Pointing morals was, however,
Crabbe's substitute. Subtitled 'Or
Hero-worship', would a more
Rationally pleasing piece,
With less of oddity and caprice
In the conduct of it, come
Of this that we're embarked upon?
Hardly: morals underlined
Outrage our taste. Besides, my mind
Is far from made up in this case

About what moral we should trace
In a story that is more
Painful than I've prepared you for.
– First, the untimely death of King.
His malady was lingering,
And yet did not take very long
Once it attacked the second lung.
Then, the death of brother Matt
At twenty-three, beleaguered at
Okehampton in the inn, who trolled,
'Unlike the ladies of the old
Times', his song; 'their hue unfaded
That needed no calash to shade it . . .'
The light young tenor 'of the old
Times, the old ancient ladies' told,
Echoing in a brother's head
Cracked gaiety, the singer dead.

    A man, thus severally bereaved,
Labours not to be deceived
By smiling seas of Life, nor Art's
Flattering pledge to furnish charts.
And no such suave commitment mars
Crabbe, the realist *sans phrase* . . .
Perhaps had Johnson lived, whose pen
Tinkered with *The Village*, then
Some one had upheld the claims
Of spectacles defined by frames,
Or songs like Matthew's, set to airs
Traditional at country fairs;
But Johnson died, unwept by most,
And left, to rule the sprawling roost,
Crabbe's earnest, just, unfocussed page
As prolix model to an age
Which, fed on ornament, would brook
Pindaric Odes to Captain Cook
And, stretched on Ossian, did not shirk
Orations paced by Fox and Burke:
Splendid, sublime and fervent, strong
In argument, but long, but long.

    Apart from that, it can be shown
To have been an age much like our own;

As lax, as vulgar, as confused;
Its freedoms just as much abused;
Where tattle stole a hero's thunder,
His death a thrill, and nine days' wonder;
Where personalities were made,
And makers of them plied a trade
Profitable and esteemed;
Where that which was and that which seemed
Were priced the same; where men were duped
And knew they were, and felt recouped
By being town-talk for a day,
Their Gothic follies on display;
Where (and here the parallel
Comes home, I hope, and hurts as well)
Few things met with such success
As indignant righteousness.
    Burke's the paradigm of this,
Hissing at enormities
In India, at Westminster-hall
(Holy debauch, a free-for-all);
A man of principle, not able
(Like Fox, who had the gaming-table
To share his heart with politics)
To guard against the squalid tricks
That Tender Conscience and Just Rage
Play, when on a public stage;
Not keeping, in his fevered heart,
Passion and Principle apart;
But purchasing his never too
Much honoured sense of what was due
To private merit and indeed
Domestic virtue, by a need
To compensate for his serene
Privacies by public spleen . . .
    To King, the friend of Irish friends,
Burke gives a bed, and Jane Burke tends
His hopeless case. And King's release
Comes in that same year, in Nice,
Whither Trevenen had, with one
Other, conveyed him, to the sun.
    The Burkes had sent him; and he rode

Back to them, slowly, overshadowed
Thenceforward, always, by a sense
Of human life's inconsequence.
     No man more worthy of his trust,
It might be thought – nor, if he must
Still worship, of his worship – than
The great, good Anglo-Irishman,
Edmund Burke. Secure within
That circle, guest of Inchiquin
At Cliefden, or else entertained
At Gregories itself, he gained
Dubious information how
Iniquitous were Pitt and Howe;
How unregarded was the merit
Of Cook, of King; how to inherit
Their mantle meant he must not hope
For advancement of much scope.
At other times the conversation
Was a liberal education
In men and manners; how Lord George
Gordon, once again at large
(Though, some years before, expelled
From this circle) was impelled
By honour when for the disbanded
Mariners he had demanded,
The year before, some action such
As could have shipped them for the Dutch;
How Cowper, in *The Task*, confessed
To remaining unimpressed
By the reasons given for
Incursions on Tahiti's shore;
How fractious Barry must be borne with,
Painting lineaments of myth
For all his tantrums, the antique
Burning his style down to the Greek;
How Nollekens had little sense
Of decency, yet could dispense
With it, to mould a *busto*; how
Cagliostro made his bow;
How civil good Sir Joshua was,
And Admiral Saunders; how, across

A field from where they sat, was found
The plot of venerable ground
Where slippery Waller lay; and how
Illiberal was Pitt, was Howe . . .
    Small wonder if his head was turned,
If a renewed resentment burned
In him to sell his rusting sword
Wherever sovereigns could afford
Ensigns announcing to the gale
Citizens of the world in sail.
Bligh gets the *Bounty*, and not he;
He's pledged himself to Muscovy.

III

His End (The Battle of Viborg, 21 June 1790)

Long, splendid shadows! Cornwall, lit
Bronze in the evening, levels it
Off, and pays all; the yea or nay
Of switched allegiance, as the day
Dies on the old church-tower, seems
A dilemma of our dreams
Which, however urgent once,
Awake we need not countenance.
The gilding beams that reconcile
This antique issue, can for mile
On cloud-racked mile slant on, to reach
Amber on a Baltic beach . . .
Apollonian, reconciling
Art, that is drenched in tears, yet smiling!
Persuading us to think all's one,
Lit by a declining sun.
    Not for George Crabbe! His it is
To give untinged veracities;
And, though it's Christian, this indeed
Our baffled heroes seem to need,
Moving to their wasteful ends,
Betrayed by principles and friends –

        Cold and pain in the breast,
        Fatigue drives him to rest.

Rising, 'to open a new
Source of comfort to you'
(Writing to his wife
The last night of his life),
Captain Trevenen, sick,
Wears on no other tack,
Aware man's born to err,
Inclined to bear and forbear.
Pretence to more is vain.
Chastened have they been.
Hope was the tempter, hope.
Ambition has its scope
(Vast: the world's esteem);
Hope is a sickly dream.
And seeking, while they live,
Happiness positive
Is sinful. Virtue alone –
This they have always known –
Is happiness below.
Therefore, she is to know,
Whatever is, is right.
That solid, serious light
Shall reconcile her to
Candidacy below
For where his sails are furled,
Far from fame and the world.

Camborne's rector would have seen
Comfort in the ghastly scene,
There in the British burial-ground
In summery Kronstadt, had he found
His son so firm, and yet so meek.
So truly Christian, truly bleak
The sentiments a man should speak,
Meeting his Maker! In our eyes
A man we cannot recognize
As Burke's or King's accomplished friend,
Cowed mumbler from the sealed-off end
Of Celtic England, glares and points;
And this raw difference disjoints
Our and Elegy's specious frame,

Framing all our deaths the same
(Our loves, our worships, levelled in
The eyes of Art, that Jacobin).
　　　Lord George Gordon! he was found
Worshipful, the country round,
Some years before. Now no one hears
His civilly enounced ideas
Without reserve. But when, as host,
He gives his Radicals their toast,
'Mr Burke! who has afforded
Grounds for discussion', he's applauded.
And, sure enough, we well may find
Burke and the Jacobins of one mind,
One self-same ruinous frame, unless
We recollect that Burke could bless
Those death-bed words from one whose head
He may have turned, whom he misled:
　　　'Though Will finds worldly scope,
　　　We have no earthly hope.'
Edmund Burke had cried, 'Amen!'
And James King, and most other men.

Vancouver

Nobody's hero, George Vancouver, ever;
Never a woman in his life, and never
Given a thing but money. Out of luck
Out of mind, he saw no medal struck
To celebrate a second Captain Cook
Come home, in him. The only way he gained
Some jeering notice was by being caned
Publicly, off Piccadilly. Yes,
Some mystery there . . .biographers suppress
The incident as best they can. All told
No, no Cook. Who loved him, who extolled,
Who even liked him? An enduring glory
For Riou, Trevenen . . . that's another story;
Fierce Welshman, David Samwell made that claim.
And yet Vancouver's shouldered them out of fame.

It seems he was not likeable; he made
What friends he had by a prudential trade
Of courtesies across interpreters
With his Peruvian or Andorran betters
In Spanish-speaking California, when
He warmed to Quadra or to Lasuèn.
True, he spoke of Hergest as a friend,
Whom he had known with Cook. But Hergest's end
(One of the band, Trevenen's friend and Riou's)
Lifts the record of Vancouver's cruise
Almost to myth; it makes Vancouver look
More than ever like a ghost of Cook,
Weird revenant to North Pacific air,
A presence, and yet humanly not there.
       Oahu saw poor Hergest re-enact
A play that he had sat through once. Attacked
No one knows why, and clubbed to death, he suffered
Cook's fate in duplicate. Only the island differed,
Hawaii killed them both, as if it meant
To kill the one man twice; and then a spent
Bloodless simulacrum called Vancouver,
That went through resolute motions, was left over,
A living corpse with mortal sickness on it.
(So it proved.) The double duty done it,
Freed or placated, some one's spirit fled
The expedition and its ailing head
When Hergest died.
                   What nonsense! Still, it's queer,
The way the thing repeats itself; a mere
Re-run, let's say, as if Time struck a groove,
Stuck there, and rhymed, and then began to move
Clack-clack, and jerkily.
                          It's less than just,
This, to Vancouver. His persistent thrust
Was crucial, and to come; the dying man
Drove, and would drive, his boat-crews, and a plan
To its fulfilment on the charts. Moreover
The drive comes though, the ruthlessness. Vancouver
Was harsh, and human; rage, tongue-lashings . . . Thus,
Just thus however, Cook *redivivus*
Would run a taut ship – on his third and last,

His fatal cruise, not many weeks went past
Without Cook raging. Thus it might be shown
Even Vancouver's faults were not his own.

    The only difference was, Cook never came
Home to be caned in Conduit Street? Ill-fame,
A savage dog called Gillray, only bayed
Meat on the hoof? Not quite. He was afraid,
He must have been, Vancouver, riding home
Goitred and stiff. He knew it had to come,
Caning, or something like it. He'd transgressed
The cardinal unwritten law of caste,
Flogged the young gentlemen – it was more than Cook
Had done, or dared. And, to be brought to book
For the transgression, he'd compounded it
By flogging, of all midshipmen, a Pitt,
The dangerous puppy, Camelford! There it is:
The mystery. For these audacities
What rhyme or reason? Say he was a sadist
(Which no one says), why should that nasty twist
Have sought its objects among officers
And settled on milord? The emphasis
Is obvious, and suicidal. True,
The man had been at sea for twenty-two
Years of his forty . . . out of touch, and yet
Not just, it's plain, an old-style martinet
Of his own quarterdeck, but some one more
Conscious of what he gambled, and what for.

    What for, if not authority? High play,
With that at stake, was common in that day:
Camelford himself, in English Bay,
Antigua, in seventeen-ninety-eight
Shot a man dead, to vindicate
His dubious seniority; and for
Mutineers of Spithead and the Nore
Courts-martial daily, hangings. This in fact
Must have saved Vancouver, when attacked
By and over Camelford. Command,
The sanctity of it, had to seem to stand,
Where possible, that year. So, in disgrace
And made to feel it, he can save his face,
And Camelford is interceded with,

Bought off, or cowed. A shabby end to myth
And to a life: no trumpets, but the sly
Susurrus of accommodations by
Pitt and his placemen – Dundas, Wedderburn –
Makes hugger mugger of a chief's return.
        Theirs was the authority he wanted,
The white whip-hands. I venture he resented,
As certainly Trevenen did, the way
Cook and his services were filed away,
And by the Pitts, the Wedderburns. No doubt
The stolid Dutchman never worked it out
(He named a creek for Wedderburn), and yet
Cook was the model he would not forget,
He'd sworn as much. Thus, loyalty to Cook
Could have been what impelled him, when he took
The whip to Camelford, and challenged Pitt
And gauged the outcome, and raged through with it.

If this is special pleading, let's admit
Vancouver needs the benefit, and may claim it;
We put the best construction that we can
On an unfriendly and a friendless man.

Commodore Barry

When Owen Roe
O'Sullivan sang Ho
For the hearts of oak
Of broken Thomond, though
Weevils and buggery should
Have wormed the wooden walls
More than De Grasse's cannon,
The sweetest of the masters
Of Gaelic verse in his time,
Lame rhymester in English, served
And laurelled Rodney's gun.

Available as ever
Implausibly, the Stuart

Claimed from the Roman stews
His sovereignty *de jure*;
But Paddy, in the packed
Orlop, the *de facto*
Sovereignty of ordure,
King George's, had to hedge
His bet upon a press
Of white legitimist sail
Off Kinsale, some morning.

A flurry of whitecaps off
The capes of the Delaware!
Barry, the Irish stud,
Has fathered the entire
American navy! Tories
Ashore pore over the stud-book,
Looking in vain for the mare,
Sovran, whom Jolly Roger
Of Wexford or Kildare
Claims in unnatural congress
He has made big with frigates.

Loyalists rate John
Paul Jones and Barry, traitors;
One Scotch, one Irish, pirate.
In Catherine the Great's
Navy, her British captains
Years later refused to sail with
The Scot-free renegade. Jones
And Barry took the plunge
Right, when the sovereigns spun;
Plenty of Irish pluck
Called wrong, was not so lucky.

'*My* sovereign,' said saucy
Jack Barry, meaning Congress;
And yes, it's true, outside
The untried, unstable recess
Of the classroom, every one has one:
A sovereign – general issue,

Like the identity-disc,
The prophylactic, the iron
Rations. Irony fails us,
Butters no parsnips, brails
No sail on a ship of the line.

Notes

Homage to William Cowper.   Cowper's poem, 'On the Death of Mrs. Throckmorton's Bullfinch', in its controlled hysteria, is surely one of the most frightening poems in English.

Hypochondriac Logic.   Written 5 October 1951, this poem was probably written earlier than any other poem in this collection, except for 'Pushkin. A Didactic Poem'.

Creon's Mouse.   I commented on this poem, in relation to one by Kingsley Amis, in *Encounter*, October 1969. It was written in November and December 1951.

Mamertinus on Rhetoric, A.D. 291.   See Burckhardt, *The Age of Constantine the Great*.

Remembering the 'Thirties.   I have amended this poem in one place. When I first printed it, I gave it an epigraph from Paul Tillich: 'Courage is an ethical reality, but it is rooted in the whole breadth of existence and ultimately in the structure of being itself.'

Hawkshead and Dachau in a Christmas Glass.   I seem to remember that this poem is connected with an essay I contributed to the Dublin periodical, *The Bell*, entitled rather quaintly 'Professor Heller and the Boots'. The poem was written in imitation of Coleridge's 'Dejection. An Ode'.

Woodpigeons at Raheny.   The house at Raheny, near Dublin, was Myles Dillon's.

Jacob's Ladder.   'Jacob's Ladder' is the name of a spur of the mountain Kinderscout in the Derbyshire Peak.

Dream Forest.   Written 19 October 1954, this poem is earlier than others in *A Winter Talent*.

At the Cradle of Genius.   Suggested by Fromentin in *The Masters of Past Time*, on Rubens and (especially) Vandyck.

A Baptist Childhood. The echo of Dylan Thomas was intended.

Corrib. An Emblem. Suggested in part by a plate of Tiepolo's 'Apollo pursuing Daphne', in Berenson's *Italian Painters of the Renaissance.*

The Pacer in the Fresco. Inspired by Andrea del Sarto's wall-paintings of the life of John the Baptist, in the Chiostra dello Scalzo, Florence. The painted panels run round four sides of a square, which is small enough for one to stand in the middle and, by a turn of the head, see the Baptist's end in his beginning, and his whole career simultaneously present as in a strip-cartoon.

The Fountain. Berkeley uses the figure of a fountain at the end of his *Dialogues of Hylas and Philonous.*

Under a Skylight. I have amended the last four lines.

from *The Forests of Lithuania.* A prefatory note to this volume read:

> This poem, like the *Pan Tadeusz* of Mickiewicz, from which it is adapted, is set in Lithuania in the years 1811 and 1812. At this period Lithuania was under Russian occupation, but the sister Kingdom of Poland had been liberated by Napoleon, and Lithuanian patriots frequently escaped to join the Polish legions fighting with the Napoleonic armies as far afield as the West Indies. In 1812, when the French launched their march on Moscow, Lithuania was also briefly liberated. The poem is to be supposed written, as Mickiewicz's poem was written, by a Lithuanian in exile, twenty years later.

I have no Polish and, as some astute reviewers realized, I rely for my knowledge of Mickiewicz's masterpiece on the excellent prose translation by G. R. Noyes in the Everyman Library. Since my poem is thus not a translation, I was (and am) at a loss how to describe it. Neither 'imitation' nor 'paraphrase' will meet the case. I have always cherished the advice of Charles Brink who, being told of my quandary, affirmed that what I had written was, strictly speaking . . . a travesty.

To a Brother in the Mystery.   The poem arose out of a visit
to Southwell Minster, and a reading of Nikolaus Pevsner's
The Leaves of Southwell. But the relationship explored in the
poem is in some sort that between myself and Charles
Tomlinson.

With the Grain.   The poem is obscure. Completed on
24 July 1957, it appears to be related to a note written three
days before. Though this is a vulnerable piece of writing,
I transcribe it here:

> It is true that I am not a poet by nature, only by
> inclination; for my mind moves most easily and happily
> among abstractions, it relates ideas far more readily than
> it relates experiences. I have little appetite, only profound
> admiration, for sensuous fullness and immediacy; I have
> not the poet's need of concreteness. I have resisted this
> admission for so long, chiefly because a natural poet was
> above all what I wanted to be, but partly because I
> mistook my English empiricism for the poet's concreteness,
> and so thought my mind was unphilosophical whereas it
> is philosophical but in a peculiarly English way.
>   Most of the poems I have written are not natural
> poems, in one sense not truly poems, simply because
> the thought in them could have been expressed – at
> whatever cost in terseness and point – in a non-poetic
> way. This does not mean however that they are worthless,
> or that they are shams; for as much can be said of much
> of the poetry of the past that by common consent is
> worth reading and remembering. Nevertheless I have
> taken a decision to write no more poems of this kind,
> only poems which are, if not *naturally*, at all events *truly*
> poems throughout.
>   For a true poem can be written by a mind not naturally
> poetic – though by the inhuman labour of thwarting
> at every point the natural grain and bent. This working
> against the grain does not damage the mind, nor is it
> foolish; on the contrary, only by doing this does each **true**
> poem as it is written become an authentic widening of
> experience – a truth won from life against all odds,
> because a truth in and about a mode of experience to
> which the mind is normally closed.

My 'Obiter Dicta' is a poem which wins through to sensuous immediacy, to poetic concreteness, by asking what sort of abstractions appeal to me, and answering that question in the only possible way, by a concrete fantasy. Instead of discriminating attractive ideas from others less attractive (which is the sort of operation to which my mind lends itself most readily), I ask in that poem by what criterion I find some ideas more attractive than others. I answer that I like ideas which are *stony*. This represents (I hope) a true poem won out of precisely that which is most inimical to it, free play among abstractions.

'A Gathered Church' actually follows out the process of thus winning to the concrete though the abstract – the church I was brought up in represents itself to me in the first place as a pattern of doctrines and doctrinal cruxes; only after giving these their head, in a free play and snip-snap of ideas and distinctions, can I win through to an apprehension of Dissent as embodied and made concrete in the personality of my grandfather.

'Under St Paul's' by contrast conceals the true movement of my mind, presenting as a deduction from concrete experience what was in fact the source of the poem (the idea of Candour), to which the concrete experience of the cathedral as a building was subsequently attached, not without difficulty. Yet perhaps this is to be less than fair to myself. As in 'The Fountain' and 'Killala', the idea and the sensuous experience struck me independently, and only in the process of writing did I recognize a harmony between them, and a rightness about splicing them together in the poem. All the same by and large it is certainly true that the idea comes into my mind more readily than the sensuous experience which not only can stand, but must stand, as its symbol.

Now I am meditating an essay on the relationship between poetry and painting. Yet I feel that I shall not express in the essay what makes this complex of ideas so interesting to me. What takes my interest is something behind the ideas, something which can be expressed only, as in 'Obiter Dicta', by finding a concrete fantasy which not only expresses but truly *is* the common element in the ideas which attract me. I have a hunch that this common element has something to do with the distinction in painting between hue and tone. This distinction is still a distinction between ideas, but the ideas are a good deal less abstract than those I started with . . .

The 'Sculpture' of Rhyme. The title comes from Pound's *Hugh Selwyn Mauberley.* Some of the notions and sentiments packed into this little epitome were teased out by me years later in an essay on Michael Ayrton's 'The Maze Maker', in *The Southern Review,* Summer, 1969.

A Sequence for Francis Parkman. When this was first published, Philip Larkin in an amiable review speculated that Francis Parkman was 'one of Mr. Davie's American friends'. The historiographer Francis Parkman (1823–93) was the author of *France and England in North America,* in many volumes. A large portion of each of these poems is a cento of passages snipped from Parkman's distinguished prose. The marginal notes were designed to be an integral part of the total composition. Unlikely as it may seem, the sequence represents my response to North America on my first visit, from September 1957 to August 1958.

Barnsley Cricket Club. An early version of this poem is one for which I have some affection. (Like many in the first half of *Events and Wisdoms,* it has a remote source in Pasternak.) I give it here under its title 'July':

For work like mine, fine weather is inclement.
'Know when to stop,' breathes hoarse July,
A stalk in his blistered mouth. 'Whatever end
You seem to reach this month is fraudulent.'

He would be cool: I see his bushy tufts
Toss in their hanging ranks, or inky single
In steeps of corn promise a stone-cold shade;
And all such ovens, funnels of hot draughts!

Frigidity can every day outwit
And stone-cold stone outstrip him. But to freeze
Distress and torpor in a finished gesture,
Hard as it is, is not the half of it.

Whatever would be natural is begun
With a more troubled feeling: we've a duty,
If nothing natural bears with finishing,
To leave our work dishevelled and half-done.

Homage to John L. Stephens.   I have suppressed the second half
of this poem.

The Vindication of Jovan Babič.   I read about Babič in Vladimir
Dedijer's *Beloved Land.* I visited Yugoslavia in 1962. 'Across the
Bay' belongs to that visit, as does 'Poreč'.

Bolyai, the Geometer.   The Hungarian mathematicians Bolyai,
father and son, I first encountered in the script of a play
The Two Bolyais by Laszlo Nemeth, and an essay by the same
hand in the *Hungarian Review.*

After An Accident.   The landscape is that of Friuli, in the
north east of Italy, behind and around the city of Gemona.

Fairy Story.   Of the original poem by Pasternak, George
Katkov remarks:

> The story of St. George, as it spread through the oral
> tradition of the 'Religious poems' (*dukhovnoye stikhi*),
> sung by the Russian equivalent of minstrels, is a fusion of
> the Byzantine story of the martyrdom of St. George and
> the western version of the liberation of the 'maiden' from
> the dragon. This explains the mixed style of imagery
> in which the Russian landscape combines with a somewhat
> westernized medieval style.

In my version I have tried to reproduce this 'mixed' and
'Westernized' style, by drawing on the diction of Spenser's
Faerie Queene which itself is modelled in part on that of the
English medieval romances. I like the metre to which the
Russian prompted me.

Back of Affluence.   Written in Iowa in 1965, this poem was
suggested by a short story by Hamlin Garland, to which I
was directed by a reading of Wallace Stegner's *Wolf Willow.*

Or, Solitude. 'Or, Solitude' is the sub-title of Wordsworth's
'Lucy Gray'. Wordsworth said of his poem: 'The way in
which the incident was treated and the spiritualizing of
the character might furnish hints for contrasting the imaginative
influences which I have endeavoured to throw over common
life with Crabbe's matter-of-fact style of treating subjects of
the same kind. This is not spoken to his disparagement,
far from it . . .'. The source of my poem is Hamlin Garland's
Boy Life on the Prairie. The poem however was written in
England.

To Certain English Poets. 'Surly pluck' is what Whitman
allows to the English – in 'Song of Myself', XXXV:

> Our foe was no skulk in his ship I tell you, (said he),
> His was the surly English pluck, and there is no tougher
>   or truer . . .

Landor, however, in 'Alfieri and Metastasio' (1856) makes
Alfieri say:

> The English are innately vulgar, with some few exceptions.
> Noblemen, suspicious and invidious of untitled gentlemen,
> whose families are more ancient and more honorable than
> theirs, and who perhaps lost their fortunes and their
> station by the wars of the Plantagenets, have no reluctance
> or dislike to walk and converse with jockeys and boxers;
> from those they gather the flowers of their phraseology . . .

– and he goes on to instance, as such a 'flower', the slang
novelty 'pluck', meaning 'courage'. If we think of E. M.
Forster in *Two Cheers for Democracy* extolling the 'plucky',
might we not think that the Englishman's diminished sense
of himself and his own possibilities is accurately graphed in
the different inflections given to 'pluck' and 'plucky' by
Landor, and by Forster? (Landor and Forster, however, have
nothing to do with my poem.)

To Helen Keller. This was commissioned by the Friends of
the Library of the University of Southern California, and was
read at the annual dinner of that Association in 1969, by
Mr Charlton Heston.

An Oriental Visitor. A Japanese girl visiting England is provoked by her experiences into recalling some of the classic *haiku* of her own poetic tradition. I found them in Henderson's *Introduction to Haiku.*

England. Among the sources for this poem are Beckles Willson, *The Life of Lord Strathcona and Mount Royal* (2 vols, 1915); Thomas Simpson, *Narrative of the Discoveries on the North Coast of America; effected by the Officers of the Hudson's Bay Company during the Years 1836–39* (London, 1843); John Henry Lefroy, *In Search of the Magnetic North*, ed. G. F. G. Stanley (Toronto, 1955); D. Geneva Lent, *West of the Mountains. James Sinclair and the Hudson's Bay Company* (Seattle, 1963); Alexander Simpson, *Life and Travels of Thomas Simpson;* Vilhjalmur Stefansson, *Unsolved Mysteries of the Arctic* (New York, 1943); Douglas MacKay, *The Honourable Company* (New York, 1936).

Six Epistles to Eva Hesse. In an introductory note to the first publication of the *Six Epistles*, I explained about Eva Hesse:

> Miss Hesse, Ezra Pound's German translator and an erudite champion of Pound's poetry, was the editor of *New Approaches to Ezra Pound* (London and Berkeley, 1969), in which was reprinted some of my own writing about Pound. Because I have more reservations about Pound than Miss Hesse and the other contributors to the book, I told her so in a private letter which I found it amusing to put into verse; and this is the first Epistle that follows, in which I also have some fun with another of the contributors, my friend Christine Brooke-Rose. Both, I'm glad to say, detected the affection behind my mockery; and so I'm sure would Charles Olson have done, if he'd lived to see the use that I make of him in the Second Epistle. It's a grief to me that he didn't. One other contributor to the Pound book, Guy Davenport, is being mocked in the later Epistles when I talk about myth.

The poems were all written, light-heartedly, between September 1969 and March 1970. A main objective was to show that, despite current assumptions on both sides of the Atlantic, as much variety of time, space and action can be encompassed in one of the traditional forms of English verse as in the much vaunted 'free form' of an American tradition originating in Pound's *Cantos*. The source of the Third Epistle is *Letters of Letitia Hargrave*, ed. by Margaret Arnett MacLeod (Toronto, Champlain Society, 1947).

Trevenen. For Trevenen, see Rev. John Penrose, *Lives of Vice-Admiral Sir Charles Vinicombe Penrose and Captain James Trevenen* (London, 1850), and *A Memoir of James Trevenen*, ed. Christopher Lloyd and R. C. Anderson (Navy Records Society, 1959). Burke's tributes to Trevenen and James King are in 'Edmund Burke's Character of his Son and Brother', Appendix 1 in *The Correspondence of Edmund Burke*, Vol. VII (Cambridge and Chicago, 1968). I also consulted *Letters of Anna Seward, written between the Years 1784 and 1807* (Edinburgh, 1811); James Prior, *Memoir of the Life and Character of the Right Hon. Edmund Burke* (1st ed., London, 1824); *The Life of George Crabbe, by his Son*; Percy Colson, *Their Ruling Passions* (London, n.d.), pp. 39–90; and various volumes of *The Correspondence of Edmund Burke*. These materials and others were assembled in the thought that I might write a closet-drama; but finding, not much to my own surprise, that I had no talent for that sort of composition, I threw the subject into the only form of writing that I know about and am practised in.

Vancouver. The modern biographies of Vancouver are by George Goodwin (*Vancouver, A Life. 1757–1798*, New York, 1931), and by Bern Anderson (*The Life and Voyages of Captain George Vancouver, Surveyor of the Sea*, Toronto, 1960). Anderson describes Gillray's caricature, 'The Caneing in Conduit Street'. For Camelford, my source is *The Farington Diary*, Vol. 2, ed. James Greig (London, 1923); I have not seen *The Life, Adventures, and Eccentricities of the Late Lord Camelford* (anon., London, 1804). I consulted also *Writings of Fermín Francisco de Lasuén*, tr. and ed. Finbar Kenneally (2 vols, Washington, 1965); John Carswell, *The Old Cause* (London, 1954); James Dugan, *The Great Mutiny* (London, 1966); and the *Dictionary of National Biography* (1896–7), articles on David Samwell; on Thomas Pitt, 2nd Baron Camelford; and Alexander Wedderburn, 1st Baron Loughborough.

Commodore Barry. John Barry (1745–1803), called the father of the American Navy, was born in Ireland and came to America about 1760. 'Rodney's Glory' by Eoghan Ruadh O'Suillebhain is printed by Daniel Corkery in *The Hidden Ireland.*

Index of First Lines

Index of Titles